COACHING HIGH SCHOOL BASKETBALL

COACHING HIGH SCHOOL BASKETBALL

A Complete Guide to Building a Championship Team

Coach Bill Kuchar
with Mike Kuchar, *ESPN Magazine*

McGraw-Hill

New York   Chicago   San Francisco   Lisbon   London   Madrid   Mexico City
Milan   New Delhi   San Juan   Seoul   Singapore   Sydney   Toronto

Library of Congress Cataloging-in-Publication Data

Kuchar, Bill.
    Coaching high school basketball : a complete guide to building a
championship team / Bill Kuchar with Mike Kuchar.
        p.   cm.
    Includes index.
   ISBN 0-07-143876-9
    1. Basketball—Coaching.   2. School sports—Coaching.   I. Kuchar,
Mike.   II. Title.

    GV885.3 .K83   2005
    796.323'2—dc22

                                        2004008277

1 2 3 4 5 6 7 8 9 0   QPD/QPD 3 2 1 0 9 8 7 6 5 4

ISBN 0-07-143876-9

Interior illustrations by Randy Miyake
Interior design by Robert S. Tinnon

McGraw-Hill books are available at special quantity discounts to use as premiums and
sales promotions, or for use in corporate training programs. For more information, please
write to the Director of Special Sales, Professional Publishing, McGraw-Hill, Two Penn
Plaza, New York, NY 10121-2298. Or contact your local bookstore.

This book is printed on acid-free paper.

To my continual and everlasting source of

inspiration, encouragement, and support—my wife,

Joan Kuchar.

Throughout the many years, you have shared with me

the long hours, hard work, and sacrifices

that my life entailed.

CONTENTS

FOREWORD

Bill Kuchar has been known as a giant in New Jersey high school basketball history for more than forty years. His teams, beginning with his first head coaching job at Saint Mary's, Jersey City, have always been outstanding offensive clubs with great balance and a fundamental base unlike any other team we faced.

As a shooting instructor, Bill is second to none. His ideas and drills for developing shooters could be readily seen in the great players he mentored, including Jim Boylan and Gary Witts. The technique and form of a Bill Kuchar–coached jump shooter was flawless.

Bill's coaching style has always been player-friendly. He has developed outstanding players and teams while forging lifetime friendships and an immeasurable camaraderie with the young men he so greatly influenced.

As a young coach in the early 1970s, my goal was to compete with Bill, and he was the standard I set for myself and my teams at Saint Anthony's. He set a very high standard for his coaching peers to strive for, and I am obliged to say he has been a personal friend as well as a mentor to me for the past thirty years.

BOB HURLEY, SR.
Head Coach
St. Anthony's High School
Jersey City, New Jersey

PREFACE

I recently concluded forty years coaching varsity high school basketball. Now that my life has gotten a little quieter, I assumed I would do what all competitors eventually do—write about their experiences participating in the game they love and share their knowledge of the game with those who desire to become better. Everything in this book has been battle tested. Because it will no longer have a bearing on my career, I have held nothing back. Although my coaching philosophy has changed over the years, I was, am, and always will be a student of the game and will continue to aspire to improve my coaching and leadership abilities year after year. Even after my retirement, I strive to never stop learning.

I consider this book essential reading for coaches of all levels who want to enhance their coaching knowledge and keep abreast of the constantly changing face of basketball. During my forty years of coaching, my thirst for basketball knowledge was never quenched. I own and have read more than a hundred books on coaching basketball. I have a video collection of more than fifty tapes, both visual and audio. I have attended countless basketball clinics all over the metropolitan and surrounding areas.

Perhaps it was my competitive nature reminding me that someone out there was working harder than I was, so I continuously pushed myself to accumulate as much knowledge about this game as possible. For example, in the beginning of my career I believed that the best defense was a great offense. My specialty was teaching the fundamentals of shooting. This eventually helped develop twenty-six 1,000-point scorers. We stressed jump shooting, pick and rolls, backdoor cuts, and the fast break. Many years ago, at a seeding meeting for a county tournament, I overheard one of the other coaches talking about my team. "They have a great offense, but think how tough they would be if they had a good pressure defense," I remember him saying. It was then I decided that I would force myself to learn man-to-man defense and become a student of defensive philosophies.

Everything that has contributed to my success as a varsity basketball coach is in this book. From the opening tap play to the end of the game, everything is covered and enhanced. It's up to you to put it all to use. The ball is in your court. Enjoy.

ACKNOWLEDGMENTS

I owe something to every assistant coach who worked for me. Therefore, it is necessary to express particular gratitude to Joe Pope, Pete Romano, Rich Lee, and Howard McCallen. I would also like to give a special thanks to my nephew, Mike Kuchar, an accomplished writer, who edited, typed, and proofread the manuscript.

KEY TO DIAGRAMS

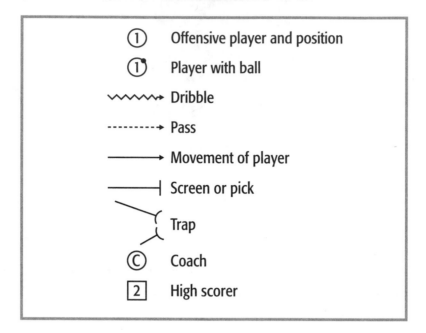

①	Offensive player and position
①	Player with ball
⌇⌇⌇➤	Dribble
------➤	Pass
⟶	Movement of player
⟞	Screen or pick
⟨	Trap
Ⓒ	Coach
☐2	High scorer

CHAPTER

1

STARTING FROM SCRATCH

Mastering the Basics of Basketball Fundamentals

Like most coaches, as a child I was an avid sports fan—whether it was basketball, baseball, football, hockey, or soccer—I loved the art of competition in sports. In fact, competition itself is an art form. You mold it and shape it into how it can fit your lifestyle and how it can work for you. Most important, I enjoyed the cold reality of testing my skills against an opponent's. It's that one-on-one camaraderie that makes athletics what it is. Growing up in Jersey City, I played all sports, and though basketball was always my first love, I tried to learn as much as possible about other sports.

During the 1970s, I used to enjoy watching Tom Landry coach the Dallas Cowboys in the National Football League. I have a genuine respect for successful coaches and admired the way he handled his players, the press, and his staff. Landry was someone I looked up to, and I wanted to model my coaching style after his. I remember when, during the start of the Cowboys' training camp in August, a reporter asked Tony Dorsett, the star running back, "What did you guys do today in practice? What did you work on?" Dorsett answered without hesitation, "Well, Coach Landry taught us the proper stance and how to hold on to the ball." Imagine that. One of the most talented, seasoned players in the league at that time, and Landry was teaching him things you're supposed to learn in Pop Warner. That is what I admired about the guy. He was a teacher of the basics; he took nothing for granted. Because he recognized how important fundamentals are, he made sure he worked on that aspect of the game.

The same is true in high school athletics. The most important aspect to teach is fundamentals. Not to downplay any other part of the game, but this is where a coach has to keep players sharp. Regardless of the game you're playing, it is the "how-to" of organized sports. As coach, you want to give them a good base of technical knowledge on how to play the game. It's never what you do when executing a play on the court; it's how you do it. There is a right way and a wrong way to do everything, and your job as a coach is to instruct your players how to do things the right way. Eventually, you will provide them with excellent habits and routines that they can carry over to the next level of play, if they choose to move on. There is no greater glory than when you have five players on the court at the same time who are fundamentally sound. Only good things will happen. You will need those fundamentals when the game is on the line.

Unfortunately, fundamentals are not easy to maintain. In fact, they are the first to fall by the wayside when a player starts thinking he is bigger than the game. This is a problem that stems from professional basketball and runs downhill. Think about it. How many times do we see, in NBA games, players not boxing out or chasing down a loose ball? How many times do we see seven-foot centers slouching on defense and not getting back to play the ball down the court? How many times do we see shooting guards throwing up ridiculous low-percentage shots past the three-point line? With the offensive expectations and elaborate fanfare saturating professional basketball these days, we rarely see well-played, disciplined basketball at that level. The purity is taken out of the game, and the fundamentals take a back seat to how many points are scored, how many dunks are made, or how many times a player works his man over on a crossover dribble. Nowhere do we take into account how many times a player might have turned the ball over or how many shots were actually missed.

So, in high school, fundamentals are the foundation, the structure that you build championships on. Kids need discipline at this level, and working the fundamentals with them every day, every practice, will provide your squad with the self-control to win games. You can't control how they are going to play when you are gone, but for the four years you have them, you must be responsible for them learning the basics of the game. Teaching methods and procedures change, but the bottom line is, the only way they learn is through repetition, drilling these techniques into players' minds every day of practice for the entire season. In hindsight, I can truly say that, in my forty years of working in basketball, coaching the fundamentals that I will discuss later in this chapter has been the most vital part of my job and has proved to be the most rewarding part as the years went on, and I watched how players developed.

As a coach, before the start of every season, there were some fundamentals I wanted to stress and made sure I covered. Usually, we did these every day, at least for the first four to five weeks of the preseason, before game planning took up a majority of our practice plan.

CUTTING BACKDOOR

I am an advocate of the backdoor rule in basketball. Almost everything I learned about this is in some way a reflection of Pete Carrill, the legendary former basketball coach at Princeton University. We worked on this relentlessly. It is an art form that, if perfected, is very difficult for an opponent to overcome. We came up with a very simple rule: If the offensive player takes two steps toward the basket, he must continue with the backdoor cut, and the passer must pass the ball if he is open. This rule will eliminate any type of turnover.

WORKING OFF PICKS OR SCREENS

Many times, players grow comfortable setting useless or unnecessary picks to free up their teammates. When working off picks, either front or back, we teach our players to walk their defensive player toward the pick before they even receive the ball. Then, we tell them to flash off the pick for the ball or cut to the basket. This way, the pick is already set up and the player can continue to make his scoring move once he gets the ball, without wasting any time.

FREE YOURSELF

It was Celtics-great John Havlicek who said, "Always move without the ball." Against pressure on an inbounds pass play, we constantly work on the aspect of "freeing yourself" for the ball. One of the ways we teach this is to run directly at the defender (nose to nose) and then cut away to receive the ball instead of moving directly at the ball when the whistle blows. This tends to work because the time to react is too short, so the defender cannot get there in time.

DEFENSIVE FLICK

This is more of a defensive technique when trailing the offensive ball carrier up the court. What we try to do is work at attacking the ball from behind. We call it "flicking" because we use the closest hand to the player to flick the ball away and into the direction of one of our players. This is a drill that works both defensive reaction and offensive awareness, so we tend to do it as much as possible. It actually sharpens our ball-handling skills.

FRONTING

In our first state championship finals, we were a fourteen-point underdog. The team we were playing had the best shooting guard in the state of New Jersey. He was averaging close to a ridiculous forty points a game. Among his other skills, he was known for an outstanding jump shot and excellent penetration to the hoop. I had an idea. I told my best defensive player to play three feet from him, and, as he went up for his jumper, to jump with him with both hands up. This became known as "fronting." Our other players were told that if he faked the shot, to position their feet and draw a charge. His first four shots were fronted and were air balls. We were up eight to nothing in the first two minutes of the game. When this player decided to fake his shot and drive, we drew three charges in the first quarter alone. The scheme worked. He wound up fouling out of the game with five minutes left in the fourth quarter. He scored only twenty points, and we won our first state title.

BOXING OUT

Boxing out is, without question, the most important defensive fundamental. Unfortunately, it is also one of the most overlooked fundamentals. It is vital to get defensive positioning and not allow second shots. Yet few teams these days at any level actually box out correctly. We used to stress this repeatedly. Our first rule is that when the offensive team shoots, all our players yell "box" and go after their man. We teach our players to make contact with their player, grow wide with their elbow up, and turn their heads toward the baseline. If the opponent goes baseline, slide in front of him. If you don't see him move in the other direction, make contact, then release and go for the ball. We made sure our assistant coaches kept an eye on this throughout the course of the game. If our players, especially our frontcourt, were not boxing out, we would immediately take them out of the game and talk with them. This would usually cure the problem.

Avoiding the Box-out

Just as boxing out can be a practiced art form on defense, avoiding the box-out on offense can also be perfected. This can be an invaluable asset to a player. Not only can he learn how to position himself to receive the ball after a missed shot. But if he learns the technique well enough, he will be in perfect position to put the ball back in the basket. We teach a player that if he intends to go to the left of the player boxing to go out after the shot goes up, tap his right side as a decoy, and then throw his right arm past his left arm, using his elbow for leverage, and get right inside his box-out.

ALWAYS MEET THE BALL

One of the things we do in every practice is run passing drills on meeting the ball. Simply meeting the ball on a pass instead of waiting until it comes to you is the best way to prevent turning over the ball on offense. It is a simple fundamental that can become a tremendously beneficial habit, once mastered. Whenever we would scout a team, we would jot down the numbers of the players who did not come and meet the ball. At practice the next day, we would tell our players who to look for on defense to create a steal.

PICK UP ALL OUT-OF-BOUNDS BALLS

This is something of a trick of the trade I picked up in my years of coaching. When the ball goes out of bounds on a possession, it is purely a way to confuse officials who have to make a quick decision but are unsure which team has possession of the ball. In this situation, we try to make the decision for them. We told our players to go to the ball and pick it up as soon as it goes out of play. It is surprising how many times officials will grant your team possession. In my forty years of coaching, I did this plenty of times and was never issued a warning for doing so.

ALWAYS STOP THE BALL FROM ADVANCING

On defense, we teach two stops. First, we try to tie up the rebounder to prevent a quick outlet pass and thereby prevent a fast break. Second, if a player is dribbling up court, the nearest defender is to pick him up and force him toward the sidelines and away from the middle. Just like most secondary defenders do in football, we use the sidelines as an extra defender. Once our trapping game is set up, we are able to put pressure on the offense by cornering them, which will usually cause the opponent to pass the ball erratically.

USING YOUR ELBOW ON DRIVES TO THE LANE

When on offense, we teach our guards or forwards to penetrate into the lane for a basket. It makes sense to drive the opposite elbow up to draw a foul on the defense. If a player is driving right, his left elbow should be up, to protect himself and draw the foul. Likewise, a player's right elbow should be up when driving left. Not only will this usually draw contact and put the player out on the line for an easy two points, but it will also give him enough protection to get the ball in the hoop. A minor bump or hit should not prevent a player from making the basket.

SETTING A PICK

Early in the preseason, we teach our players this fundamental. The pick is another invaluable trait to have as a player, enabling teammates to get free to score. We teach our kids to "get big" on picks. We want their shoulders square, their heads up, their chests expanded, and their feet set. As coach, show players how to hold their wrists to prevent any stray hand movements that may end up as fouls. Another point to remember is to cover the groin, preventing the likely cheap shot that often comes

for setting a strong pick. The key is that, while most players will set a pick directly behind the player in his blind spot, we teach our players to set the pick halfway in the direction that the defensive player will turn into. We try to outsmart our defenders by beating them to the spot that they will eventually have to reach.

ODDS AND ENDS

A coach should stress thirty other key fundamentals early in the season:

1. Never leave your man on defense unless the ball leaves his fingers.
2. When receiving an outlet pass, pivot to avoid a charge.
3. The rebounder must pivot before passing to outlet.
4. On pressure defense, count five seconds for the official when your man has the ball. It keeps him aware that you know the rules.
5. Always pick up an out-of-bounds ball.
6. On offense, the screener is always open.
7. On offense, look for the defender before making a pass.
8. Anticipate passes and always look to draw charges. At the end of each season, we present a trophy to the player who drew the most charges.
9. When creating a fast-break opportunity, stop at the foul line and use a bounce pass for the man cutting to the hoop. Never use a chest pass; it's easy to pick off.
10. When jumping for a rebound, time your jump. You want to catch the ball at its highest point off the rim.
11. Create space when coming down with the ball on a rebound by swinging your hips while planting your feet. You would be surprised at how many people will stay out of your way.

12. When playing a rebound on offense, anticipate the outlet pass to the sides of the floor. Guards should look for steals while forwards and centers tie up the rebounder.

13. Leverage: On defense your head must be lower than your offensive players.'

14. Never dribble down the court and shoot anything except a layup without making at least one pass.

15. Never go for pump fakes on defense. Keep your feet on the ground unless the ball is already in the air, then block it.

16. If you are going to use an intentional foul, make sure you hit or grab the player's shooting arm or go for a steal.

17. Never foul on a difficult shot.

18. On defense, always point one hand at your man and one at the ball.

19. Pivot out of defensive pressure by putting your elbow in the player's face.

20. Be calm against pressure and move the ball.

21. Don't reach with contact. It is a foul.

22. If the rebounder brings the ball down, take it off him.

23. Always spin when being boxed out.

24. Open your hips to the ball on all backdoor cuts.

25. Hold wrist when screening to prevent fouling.

26. Always meet the ball.

Plus four kinds of dribbling techniques:

27. Control dribble: Bend low, dribble with opposite hand protecting the ball, and keep your elbow up.

28. Speed dribble: Ball should be off to your side, not in front of you.

29. Change-of-pace dribble: Drag left foot, then drop left shoulder and accelerate when player is up and not in a defensive stance.

30. Crossover dribble: Change direction, drag left foot to prevent striking the ball.

THE SWEETEST SOUND

Establishing the Mechanics That Will Lead to Uncanny Accuracy of a Dead-On Jump Shot

There is no substitute for excellent shooting, which is why I decided to start this book with this facet of basketball. There is no question that good shooting, when executed correctly, is the most important part of the game. All the successful teams in this game, at any level—high school, collegiate, or professional—have one thing in common—excellent shooters. But we should realize one simple fact: shooters aren't born with "dead-on" jump shots. They develop them. In fact, it is the only part of the game that you can practice alone. Although people say, "Practice makes perfect," I disagree. In my opinion, "perfect practice" makes perfect. If you want to become a great shooter, you must master the fundamentals and basics of shooting. In this chapter, you will find out all you need to know about properly shooting a basketball.

All my teams, regardless of their win-loss record, were among the best shooting teams in the state, based on their excellent percentage. Early in our practice season, I stressed the fundamentals of shooting. I split the team into two groups and sent them to the six baskets in our gym. While each pair was shooting a set number of foul shots and jump shots, I rotated from one basket to the next and pointed out the correct techniques of shooting. This is what I call my collaborative learning process in practice—the player who isn't shooting coaches the other player on the techniques I taught while he was taking his shots. In other words, the players become the coach. This way, each player learns from his own mistakes and those of his teammates. Plus, I have twelve assistant shooting coaches, just like that!

This technique takes a while to pick up, but once players get it, the system moves quickly. Doing this every day enabled me to just split up the groups. My technique was to do this for fifteen minutes at the beginning of practice. Although this may be considered an "old-school" approach to teaching, a coach who instills the proper attitude and demeanor in the team will have players who want to help each other and take practice seriously. This is why I start from the beginning of the season—it forces players to learn to work with each other and learn from each other. An immeasurable bond of trust and communication is formed early on, something that grows stronger as the season goes on.

Many teams suffer from what I consider to be my "Murphy's Law" in shooting—forcing shots. I established a rule against forced shots, taking any player who threw up a ridiculous, or very low percentage, shot—except at the end of the half—out of the game for a couple of minutes. This was a great method of positive reinforcement. Players quickly learned not to force a shot again.

Basically, I've developed my own ten golden rules of shooting, and they deal with each of the techniques that must be mastered to become a great shooter.

1. *Position the ball:* Your hand should be centered on the ball, and the ball should be lying in your palm. If you are a right-handed shooter, your left hand should be to the side of the ball and should not interfere with the shot—

Figure 2.1 Correct

Figure 2.3 Wrong

Figure 2.2 Wrong

2. *Position the elbow:* Your shooting elbow should always be close to your body and under the ball. If your elbow is away from your body, your follow-through will not point to the basket, and you could block the vision of your right eye (fig. 2.4). In Figure 2.5, the ball is blocking the vision of the right eye and the follow-through will not point to the basket. These are common mistakes among inexperienced shooters.

it should only be used as a guide (fig. 2.1). Many young players think that the guide hand plays an integral part in the shot, but it doesn't (fig. 2.2). The incorrect way to hold the ball is to form a bridge with the fingers and hold the hand too far back, with the shooting hand too far to the right (fig. 2.3).

Figure 2.4 Correct

Figure 2.5 Wrong

Figure 2.7 Wrong

3. *Wrist and fingertip control:* Your wrist should be cocked, with your elbow parallel to the ground. When shooting, flip your wrist and point to the basket. Your arms do not shoot the shot; use your fingertips and wrist only (fig. 2.6). In Figure 2.7, the wrist is not cocked— the elbow is out. It is the incorrect way of shooting.

Figure 2.8 Correct

Figure 2.6 Correct

4. *Follow-through:* After taking the shot, hang your hand extended and point to the basket. I taught my players to hang your hand for two seconds or until the ball goes in (fig. 2.8). This way you are forcefully willing the shot in. Do not cut short your follow-through, and do not point your follow-through away from the basket. The perfect picture of this is Michael Jordan's

Figure 2.9 Wrong

Figure 2.10 Wrong

winning jump shot in the 1997 NBA championship. You see him release the ball with perfect spin and a great follow-through. He keeps his hand up until the ball goes through the net. Figure 2.9 shows a short follow-through; the arm is not completely extended. Figure 2.10 is also incorrect, because the wrist should not flip to the left, but should point directly to the basket.

5. *Arch the ball:* You want to get a nice arch on the ball, not shoot a line drive. Therefore, the angle of your arm is very important. I told my players to picture themselves in a phone booth. You want your arm to rise upward on the shot, not outward (fig. 2.11).

Figure 2.11 Correct

Figure 2.12 Wrong

Figure 2.13 Wrong

In Figure 2.12, the end result will only be a line-drive shot. You'll be able to develop an excellent arch on your shot if you use your arm correctly.

6. *Radar eyes:* Always keep your eyes on the rim, never on the ball (fig. 2.13). Too many young players develop the bad habit of watching the flight of the ball as it leaves their hands (fig. 2.14).

Figure 2.14 Wrong

Figure 2.15 Correct

Figure 2.16 Wrong

7. *Proper spin:* Use your fingertips to give you that picture-perfect, north-to-south, end-over-end spin (fig. 2.15). A sidespun ball will spin off the rim (fig. 2.16).

Figure 2.17 Correct

8. *Aim for the back part of the rim:* Ninety percent of missed shots hit the front of the rim. In the beginning of the game, aim the ball to go over the front of rim. As the game progresses and fatigue sets in, you should always aim for the back part of the rim. It is important that you learn to adjust your shot depending on how tired you are.

9. *Stay square to the basket:* So many times in games, we hear announcers say, "He squares to the hoop, he shoots. . . ." Squaring your shoulders and facing the basket before you shoot the ball is imperative. If you are shooting from a stationary position (as if you were in a zone offense), you must square to the basket before even receiving the ball (fig. 2.17). In Figure 2.18, the player's feet are not square to the basket.

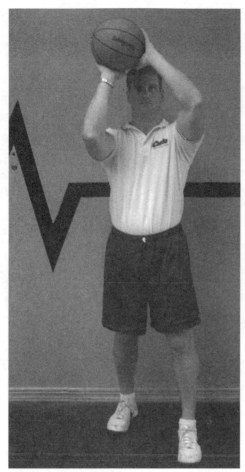

Figure 2.18　Wrong

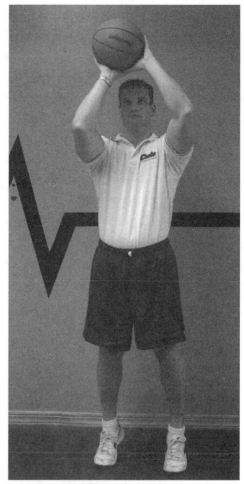

Figure 2.19　Wrong

10. *Develop the art of the jump shot:* I always had my players shoot free throws before jump shots because the two are similar. If you are dribbling, you must stop, pivot, and square to the basket before you shoot. So, essentially, you are taking a moving, instead of a stationary, free throw. Use your legs to spring you straight forward, and release the ball at the peak of your jump. Arch the ball, use end-over-end spin, and follow through, pointing to the rim, and then return to your "original footprints." By this, I mean you should come down exactly where you went up. Prevent yourself from moving sideways or back on your heels. As previously noted in Figure 2.17, besides just squaring to the basket, this shooter has mastered other fundamentals—his elbow is in and under the ball—his wrist is cocked, his left hand is on the side of the ball, and he can see with both eyes. He is ready to shoot. The incorrect way is displayed in Figure 2.19. The ball is back on the side of his head. Using mostly his arm, this will cause a heavy ball.

THE BEST SHOOTING DRILL

The best drill to practice the preceding fundamentals is to stand three feet from the rim, the ball in the palm of your shooting hand and your elbow under the ball and next to your body. Your opposite arm is at your side. Your hand should be cocked (fig. 2.20). Flip your wrist with proper spin and arch. Use fingertip control, keeping your eyes on the rim, and follow through, pointing to the rim. When you make the three-footer, step back to six feet and shoot with one hand. If you make the shot, then move again, to nine feet, then twelve feet, until you reach the foul line. The drill ends when you make two shots in a row with one hand from the foul line.

Figure 2.20

SHOOTING FUNDAMENTALS FROM A TO Z

A. Fingertips on the ball.

B. Hand spread in natural position.

C. No strain in the hand.

D. Thumb spread slightly. An upright thumb will cause the hand to collapse on the ball, sacrificing fingertip control.

E. The head, shoulders, hips, knees, and toes should face the target.

F. Your eyes should be concentrating just beyond the front of the rim.

G. The wrist of the shooting hand should be cocked.

H. If the ball was split in half, the cut line should be between the middle and forefingers of the shooting hand.

I. The arm is bent at the elbow, forming a 90-degree angle.

J. The bottom of the elbow is pointing to the floor, while the upper part of the elbow is pointing at the target.

K. The ball is slightly in front of the head, and to the side of your face. The elbow should not be outside of the ball. The ball should be almost in a direct line between the target and the shoulder.

L. The knees are comfortably flexed, with the foot corresponding to the shooting hand slightly advanced.

M. The ball is on "railroad tracks" leading directly to the target. If you push it straight along the tracks and judge the distance properly, it will go in.

N. The rim is two balls in diameter. Get the ball above the rim so it can have more of a chance of going in. A flat arc limits the points of entry.

O. Keep the nonshooting hand to the side of the ball. Don't let it interfere with the forward thrust of the ball.

P. From a sound readiness position, roll the forearm back slightly and then push up through the ball, following through completely. Your legs will straighten out, and you may even finish up on your toes.

Q. At the completion of a properly executed shot, the forearm resembles a flagpole attached to a building.

R. At the release, if the arm were made of rubber, the hand would grab the target.

S. The ball will go exactly where the hand guides it. Therefore reach directly at the target. Do not turn the hand right or left because the ball will follow your direction.

T. Start every day's shooting drill close to the basket, working back gradually. Through this time-tested method, you are constructing sound techniques and building confidence.

U. As you move farther away from the basket, don't change any of the skills discussed above. Simply increase your leg power by bending your knees.

V. During the release, do not move your head. When you do, your body jerks, pulling against the shooting arm.

W. Practice by shooting with only one hand on the ball.

X. Hold your arm completely straight up and shoot with just the hand. This is done to strengthen the hand and the wrist and to increase the "feel" in the shooting hand. This is only a drill, not a method of shooting.

Y. Shoot the ball rapidly against the board one-handed. Catch it one-handed. Do this nine times in succession and put the tenth shot in. Repeat often.

Z. Practice!

EXPLOSIVE OFFENSE

Running the Double-Motion Offense

Because of the ongoing development of solid defenders, today's coaches are always looking for ways to alleviate the pressure and demands of these defenses by installing quality motion offenses, which utilize many scoring options. The basic premise of a motion offense is for players without the ball to move away, or screen away, from the ball to get better shots.

Many coaches switch their defenses at various stages of the game. Some will switch from a man-to-man to a zone, box and one, or triangle and two setup. In any case, a quality motion offense can be used against a man-to-man, as well as all types of zones such as the box and one, triangle and two, and the diamond and one. I designed this offense several years ago, not only to combat the above-mentioned defenses but also to install an offense that would give our star scorer better-percentage shots, which would translate into higher scoring. As I discuss in this chapter, the offense is predicated on the success of the point guard, shooting guard, and small forward—those are generally known to be the three best shooters on the court.

In this general half-court 1-2-2 setup (1 is the point guard, 2 is the shooting guard), the 3-player (or small-shooting forward) is the focus of play. In either case, this motion offense presents various ways to score by the three players and, more important, puts them in the right position to make plays by using screens and cuts away from the ball. This offense will set up no fewer than four screens for your best shooter, along with scoring options for your other players as a backup plan.

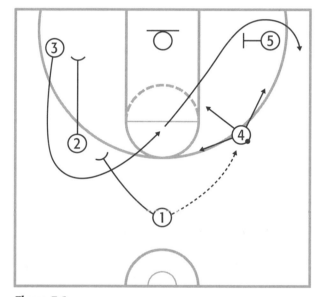

Figure 3.1

As usual, the point guard (1) will take the ball at the top of the key, call the offense, and set up the motion (see fig. 3.1).

- 1 will pass to 4 (power forward) at the right elbow, setting up the motion as 2 down-screens for 3.
- After passing to 4, 1 screens away for 3 as he curls to the foul line (option A).
- If the shot is not there, 3 rolls down to the basket.

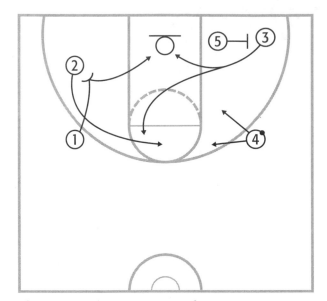

Figure 3.2 Options B, C, D, E, and F

Figure 3.3 Option G

- If 3 does not receive the ball in either of those two situations, he continues to the baseline off a screen by 5 (center), and sets up in the corner behind the three-point line (option C; see fig. 3.2).
- If these three options are unavailable, 4 looks for 1 cutting to the basket since hesitating after setting a screen for 2 (option D).
- 2 will roll off the screen and flashes to the top of the key for a three-point opportunity (option E).
- If there is no shot with these two options, 4 passes to 2 at the point, while 5 screens for 3 for possible layup (option F).

- If the layup is not there for 3, then he continues to flash to elbow where he will receive the pass from 2. This is the last phase of the motion.
- 1 will clear out of the middle (fig. 3.3)
- 5 now will up-screen for 4, who will look to cut to the basket for a possible layup (option G).

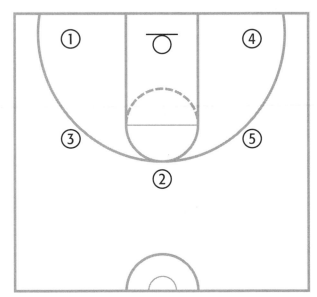

Figure 3.4 Reset Offense

- If the shot is unavailable, 3 will get the ball back to 2 and reset the double-motion offense (fig. 3.4).
- 2 will now pass to 5 to start the motion as 3 sets low screen for 1, then cuts to basket.
- 2 will screen away, setting the second pick for 1, who will roll to the foul line (option A).
- If 1 does not receive the ball in the key area, he continues to roll to the basket for a possible layup (option B).

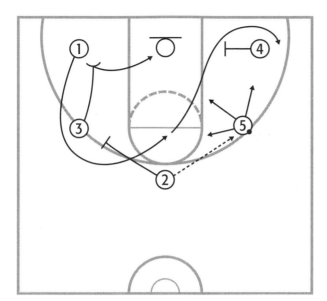

Figure 3.5 1 Becomes Prime Shooter

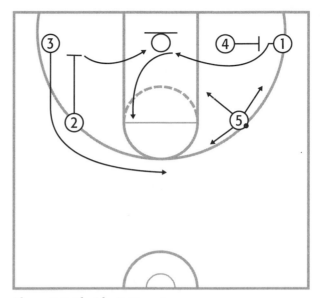

Figure 3.6 Shot by 2, 3, or 1

- If 1 does not receive the ball in either of those two situations, he continues to the baseline off-screen by 4 for possible three-point opportunity (fig. 3.5).

- Once again, if these options are not available, 5 looks for 2, who should be rolling to the basket since hesitating after setting a down-screen for 3.

- 3 will move off-screen and settle near the top of the key for a possible three-point opportunity (fig. 3.6).

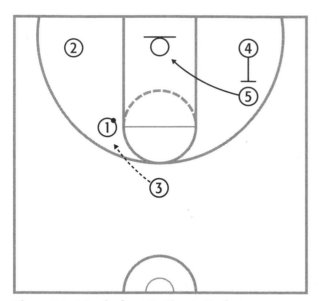

Figure 3.7 1 Looks for 5 Cutting to Basket

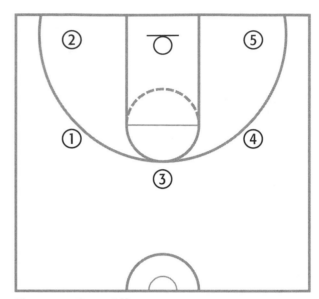

Figure 3.8 Reset Offense

- The motion starts up again. If 1 is not open for the hoop, he'll flash to the elbow, receiving the ball.
- 2 clears out of the middle.
- 4 up-screens for 5, who will roll to the basket for a possible layup (fig. 3.7).

- If the pass is not there, the offense must reset again, this time with 3 at the point. The double motion begins with 3 (fig. 3.8).

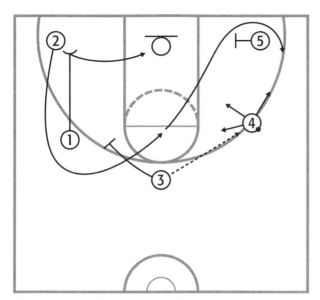

Figure 3.9 2 is the Prime Shooter

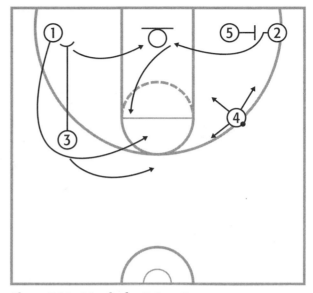

Figure 3.10 4 Looks for 3, 1, or 2

- 3 will now pass to 4 to start the offense as 1 sets a low screen for 2.
- 2 will roll off-screen from 1 and then 3, setting up at the foul line for a short jumper as 1 rolls to the basket.
- If the shot is not there, 2 will continue to roll to the hoop for a possible layup.
- If these two options are not there, 2 will continue toward baseline, off-pick from 5, and set up in the corner for a possible three-point shot (fig. 3.9).

- If 2 can't get the ball, 4 looks to 3, who rolls to the basket after hesitating since setting the pick for 1.
- 1 rolls high off-screen from 3 and sets up at the arch for a three-point shot.
- If those two shots are not there, 4 passes to 1 as 2 now curls behind pick of 5 and cuts to basket for a possible layup (fig. 3.10).

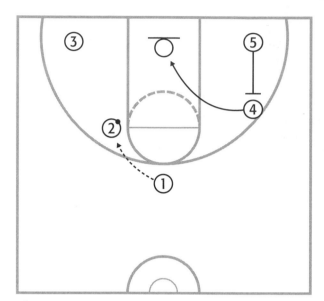

Figure 3.11 2 passes to 4

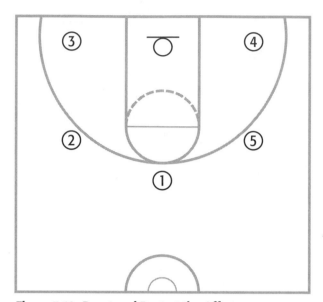

Figure 3.12 Reset and Restart the Offense

- Once again, if the last option is not available, 2 continues to flash to the elbow and will receive the ball from 1.
- 3 clears out of the middle.
- 5 will up-screen for 4, who will roll to the basket for a quick layup (fig. 3.11).

- If the shot is not available, the offense will now reset to their original formations after three complete rotations with 1 at the point, leading the offense (fig. 3.12).

Coach's Note: It is important to note that, in these three separate rotations, the 1, 2, and 3 players rotated, each either playing the point or possible three-point shooters. The 4 and 5 players set up screens and used backdoor cuts.

SIMPLE-MOTION OFFENSE

Running Two
Simple-Motion Offenses

Along with the double-motion offense, I also taught a number of other simple-motion offenses with one purpose in mind. I use the word *simple* because, although they are simple to understand and relatively easy to teach your younger players, when used correctly they can be extremely difficult for opposing teams to adjust to and to stop. For the most part, the double-motion offense was what we lived and died by, so we would use these other motion offenses as a decoy when we played against teams we hadn't seen during the regular season. Although we practiced these offenses throughout the season, we knew our opponents scouted our regular-motion offense. Come tournament time, we would simply switch to our two secondary-motion offenses to throw our opponents off guard.

Motion Offense 1 (layup or open shot at top of key)

- 1 passes to 2 as 3 sets pick for 5.
- 1 sets a pick for 3, who flashes to the top of the key for a three-point shot.
- 2 looks to pass to 5, cutting to the hoop, or to 3 at the top of the key for three-point shot
- 4 clears out (fig. 4.1).

- 3 passes to 1 as 4 sets pick for 2.
- 3 sets pick for 4, who flashes to the top of key.
- 1 looks to pass to 2, cutting to the basket, or to 4 at the top of the key.
- 5 clears out (fig. 4.2).

Coach's Note: You can continue to run this motion until they have the layup inside or the two- or three-point shot from the key area.

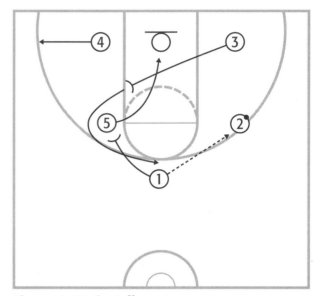

Figure 4.1 Motion Offense 1

Figure 4.2 Opposite Side

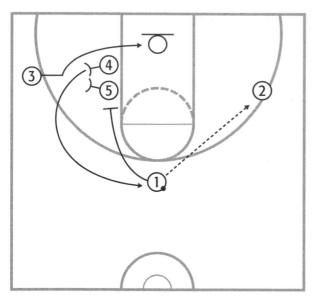

Figure 4.3 Motion Offense 2

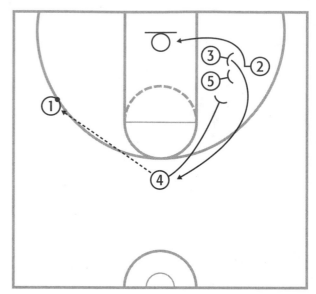

Figure 4.4 Opposite Side

Motion Offense 2
(three-point and layup and 1-3-1 motion offense)

- 1 passes to 2, then sets pick at foul line (fig. 4.3).
- 4 and 5 double-pick for 3, and 2 looks for cutting 3 toward the baseline.
- 4 cuts off double screen from 5 and 1 and flashes to three-point area.
- 2 passes to 4.

Coach's Note: If 2 is being denied pass, first option is a backdoor cut by 2, or he can go one-on-one with his defender.

- 5 crosses to opposite lane with 3.
- 4 passes to 1 and sets a foul-line pick (fig. 4.4).
- 2 cuts off double screen by 5 and 3, as 3 rolls off double screen from 5 and 4 toward the three-point area.

- 3 passes to 4 and sets a pick (fig. 4.5).
- 1 cuts off double pick from 2 and 5, and 2 flashes off double screen from 5 and 3 toward the three-point area.

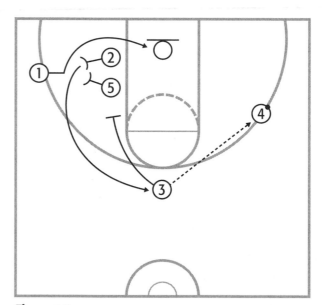

Figure 4.5

CHAPTER

5

OFF AND RUNNING

Installing the Fast Break and Full-Court-Press Offenses That Will Get Down Court in a Hurry

One of the first things that coaches look at when evaluating their talent in the preseason is overall team speed. There is no substitute for team speed, which can be an immeasurable asset to your program. Speed is one common denominator for all successful teams, whether in high school, college, or the National Basketball Association. Teams in the higher echelon of the NBA today—teams like the San Antonio Spurs, the Los Angeles Lakers, and the New Jersey Nets—all have excellent speed and can get down court quickly.

The fast break is one of the best-known tools in basketball. If you have the talent to get down the court and score points in a hurry, why not use it? The key to running the right fast break is to create mismatches. You want to see three-on-twos, three-on-ones, or two-on-ones all in your favor. As simplistic as it may sound, there is a lot more to running a successful fast break than just grabbing a rebound and running the length of the court. It has to be coached and taught. Just like any other offense, players have to be in the right spots to work the break completely.

As a coach, I installed one fast break and several different press offenses. My goal was to give my opponent as many different looks as possible—the last thing I wanted was for them to sit back and get comfortable in a zone. Naturally, when teams started to realize we were setting up the fast break directly after a rebound, they would stay at our end of the court after a basket and press us. When they tried to full-court-pressure us, we had ways of breaking the press and getting the ball down court in a hurry using ball movement and player positioning. To do this, we had to teach all our players to rebound the ball and push it up court.

PEACOCK BREAK

In 1969, the Duke University men's basketball team, which was ranked in the top twenty-five in the country and was getting tremendous national acclaim at the time, came to Jersey City, New Jersey, to play the Saint Peter's College Peacocks in a regular-season game. St. Peter's put on a fast-break clinic and beat Duke by thirty points. What I describe here is the same pattern of the fast break that St. Peter's used to upend Duke. We had tremendous success using this pattern. When we first installed it, we tried to stay as formal as we could with the original setup, but through the years I added some adjustments to the way it is run. Although this is a simple fast-break pattern, it takes a lot of communication and practice to run it efficiently.

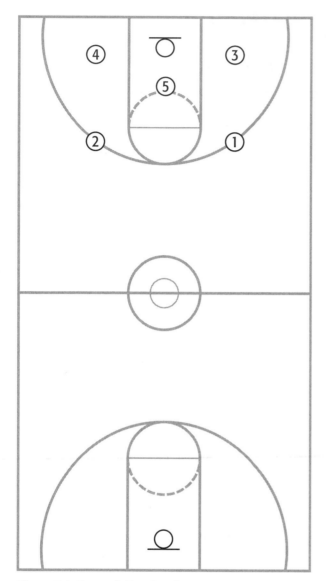

Figure 5.1 Peacock Fast Break

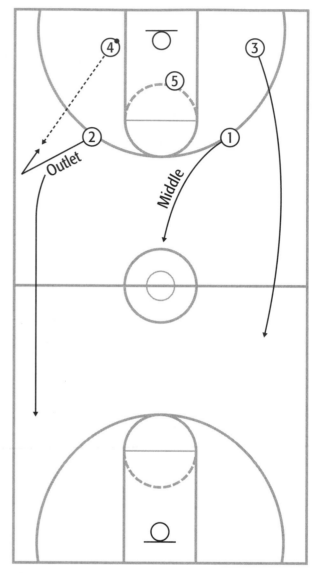

Figure 5.2 Ball-Outlet-Middle

- The original setup is much like a 2-3 zone, but we run this fast break while in a zone or man-to-man (fig. 5.1).
- Either 3, 4, or 5 can start the break. In Figure 5.2, 4 is shown rebounding and starting the break.
- When he gets the rebound, he yells "Ball," telling 2 to flash out to the side (area key extended) to take the outlet pass.
- 4 throws a two-handed over-the-head pass to 2, who comes to meets the ball.

- 1 flashes to midcourt and yells "Middle" to receive the pass from 2, starting the fast break.
- 3 sprints to fill the third lane.

Coach's Note: If 2 receives the pass from 4 and no one is in the middle at half-court, 2 then dribbles to midcourt and 1 and 3 sprint down the sides, each taking a lane. The guard starting the fast break must always stop at the foul line if the defenders get back.

The key words are: *ball, outlet, middle.*

THE FALCON OFFENSE

The full-court man-to-man-press Falcon offense will work consistently against a man-to-man press defense. To beat any pressing defense, a team must spread the court and move the ball. It must limit any type of dribbling. One of our most important rules was to never pass back; always pass ahead. By passing back, a team has to beat the press twice because an opponent will set up a trap wherever players move to. Also, we always tried to turn our Falcon pressure offense into a fast break by spreading three lanes and keeping the ball in the middle of the court so teams cannot use the out-of-bounds lines as a trap. In this setup, 5 always releases early to get a head start down court while 4 is the trailer.

- 5 makes an early release down court.
- If a shot is made, 4 takes out the ball.
- 1 sets a pick for 2 (fig. 5.3).

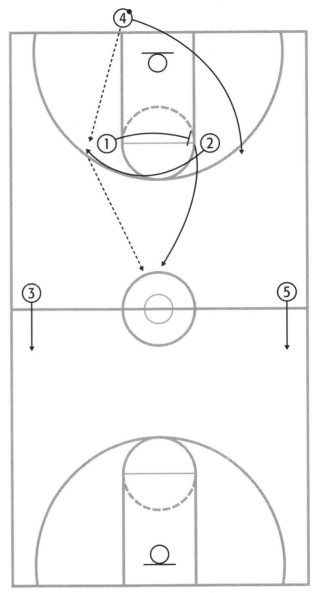

Figure 5.3 Falcon Offense, First Option

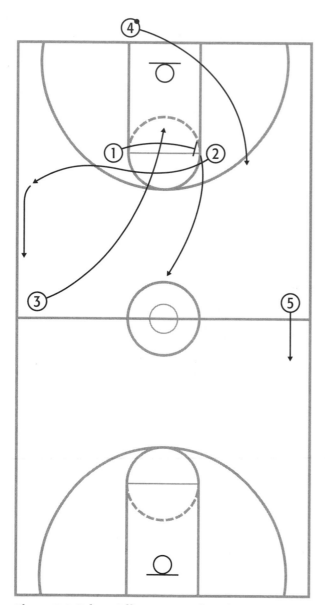

Figure 5.4 Falcon Offense, Second Option

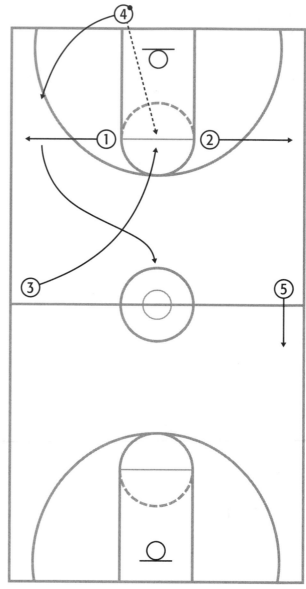

Figure 5.5 Falcon Offense, Third Option

- 1 flashes to midcourt.
- 4 passes to 2.
- 2 passes to 1.
- Start fast break as 4 trails behind lane.
- If 2 is covered, he flashes to 3 position.
- 3 cuts to the middle for the ball (fig. 5.4).
- 3 passes to 1, 2, or 4 to start fast break.

- 1 and 2 split sides of court.
- 4 passes to 3 (fig. 5.5).
- 1 flashes to the middle and gets pass from 3.
- 4 replaces 1, and fast break is started.
- 3 and 5 cut to foul line extended.
- 1 sets pick for 2.

Coach's Note: This option is used if 2 is covered. 2 takes 3's place as 3 cuts for a pass from 4.

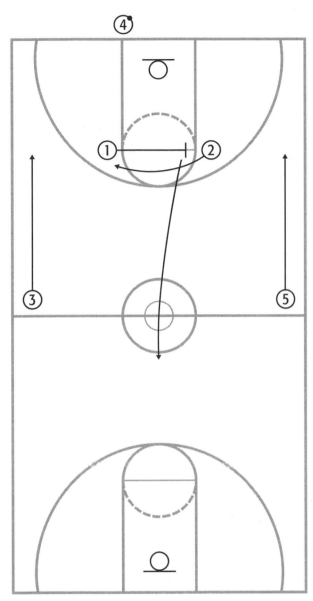

Figure 5.6 Atom Option

- 1 sets pick for 2
- 1 flashes for long baseball pass from 4 for layup (fig. 5.6).

Coach's Note: We use this option as a game winner and call it the Atom option.

UCLA: FULL-COURT MAN-TO-MAN AND ZONE-PRESS OFFENSE

Hall-of-Famer John Wooden, the former UCLA basketball coach and arguably the best teacher of basketball ever, used this type of fast break early in his career. One of his favorite maxims was, "Be quick, but don't hurry," meaning, make sure you react quickly and get down the court, but don't get sloppy by hurrying down the court and committing costly turnovers. After watching plenty of his games and analyzing how the Bruins ran this offense, we used the same basics but threw in a couple of options and additional rules.

It is vital to work on this type of offense early in the season to give your players time to get accustomed to running it. My custom was to store this away until one of our most important games of the year, when teams expected us to run either the Falcon or Diamond offense.

- 1 cuts and stops at weak-side foul line extended.
- 2 cuts and looks for pass from 3 at the foul-line area.
- If 3 passes to 2, 1 flashes to half-court circle and gets pass from 2 (fig. 5.7).
- 1 starts the break at midcourt, with 4 and 5 on the wings.
- 3 cuts and fills the open lane in the event that 2 cannot pass to 1.

Coach's Note: Middle guard must always stop at the foul line on the fast break, unless he has a two-on-one situation.

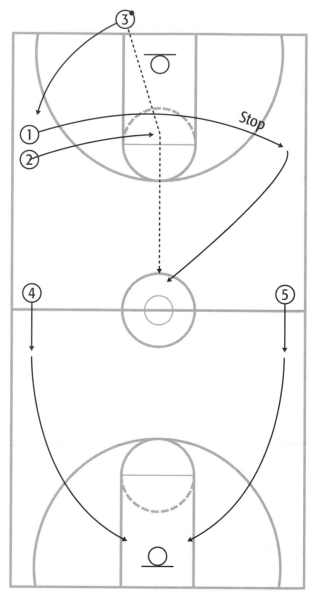

Figure 5.7 UCLA, First Option

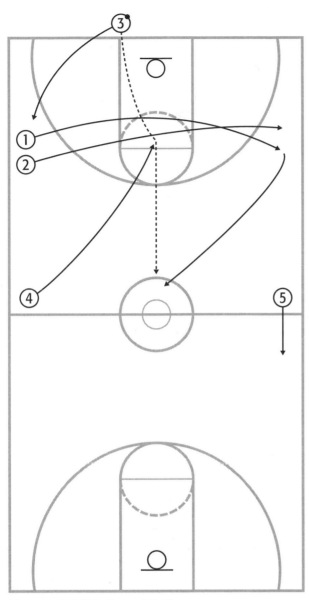

Figure 5.8 UCLA, Second Option

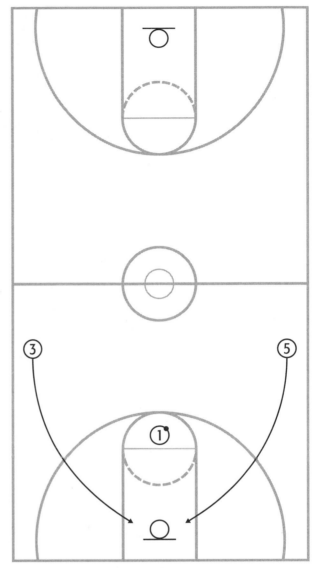

Figure 5.9 UCLA, Third Option

- 1 cuts across court, then 2 cuts across court.
- If 2 is not open, 1 cuts to half-court circle.
- 2 stops weak-side foul line extended.
- 4 flashes up the middle for pass from 3.
- 3 passes to 4 (fig. 5.8).

- 3 fills the open lane.
- 4 passes to 1.
- 3-1-5 start fast break (fig. 5.9).
- 1 always stops at the foul line.

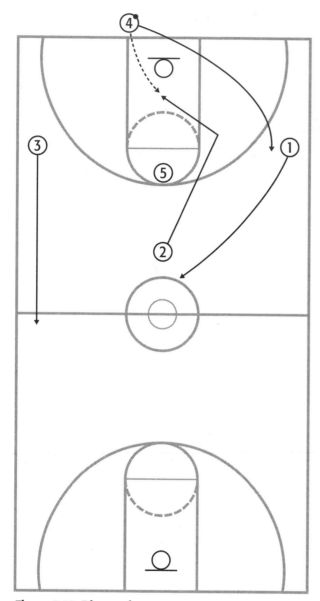

Figure 5.10 Diamond

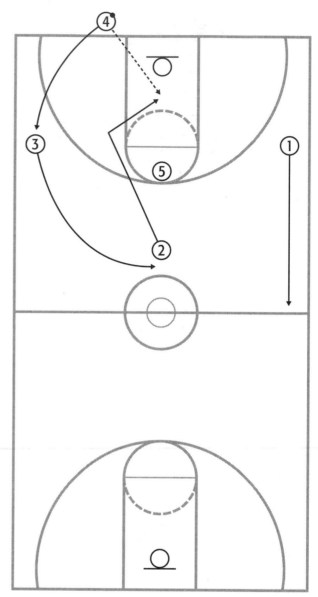

Figure 5.11 Opposite Side

DIAMOND: FULL-COURT-PRESS OFFENSE

The Diamond is a full-court zone-press offense. This is a relatively simple offense with some basic rules:

1. Do not pass back.
2. Move the ball quickly without dribbling.
3. Spread the court.
4. Get the ball into the middle.

5. Form three lanes and go into a fast-break offense.
   - 4 passes to 2.
   - 1 flashes to middle as 4 replaces 1 (figs. 5.10 and 5.11).
   - 2 passes to 1, 3, or 4 to start fast break.

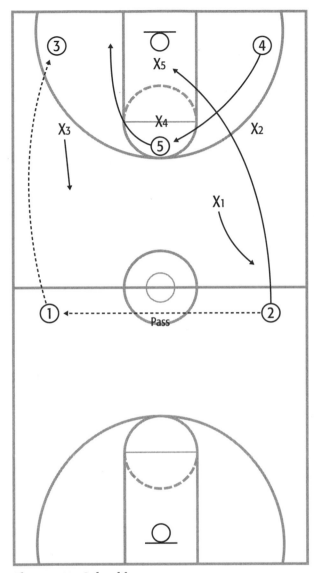

Figure 5.12 Columbia

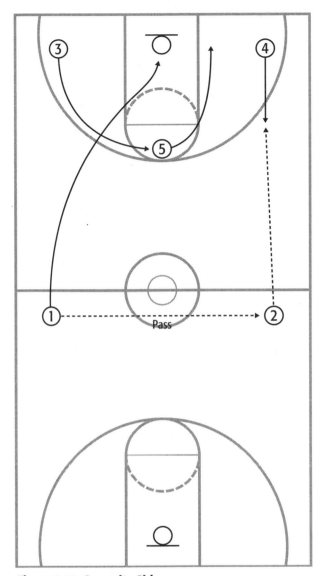

Figure 5.13 Opposite Side

COLUMBIA HALF-COURT ZONE-PRESS OFFENSE

This offense is patterned against a 1-3-1 half-court trap defense. The most important rule is the rule of "first pass entry." Both guards stop three feet from the half-court line in the backcourt. If the defender guarding the point guard is committed to playing him on one side, either right or left, the point guard quickly passes to the 2-man, who then passes across the court back to the point guard.

In 1996, we added another option for our state championship game against a powerful preparatory school. Our 2-guard split the defenders and dribbled toward the foul line, looking to penetrate and pass inside or take the foul-line jump shot. This particular player scored forty-one points, sixteen from the foul line, as we upset a more talented team.

- 1 and 2 stop in backcourt in the ten-second area.
- 2 quickly passes the ball to 1 as X3 moves up with 1.
- 1 passes over the top to 3.
- 5 rolls to ball-side low post as 4 flashes to the top of the key (figs. 5.12 and 5.13).

- 2 flashes to the hoop.
- 4 can pass to 5 or 2 or shoot inside the key.
- 2 splits the seam between X1 and X3 and quickly dribbles to the foul-line area.
- 5 rolls down to ball-side low-post area.
- 4 flashes to opposite post.
- 3 flashes to three-point area (fig. 5.14).

Coach's Note: 2 can either shoot, pass to 4 or 5 on the post, or kick the ball out to 3 for a three-point shot.

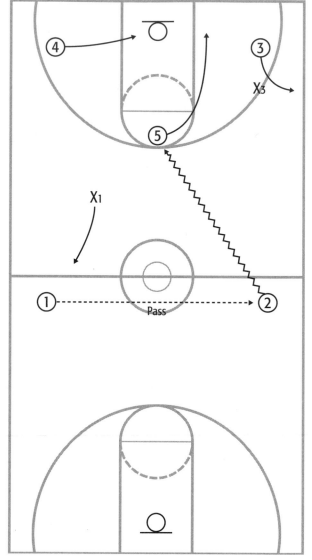

Figure 5.14 Columbia (Dribble) Option

OUT-OF-BOUNDS AND LAST-SECOND PLAYS

Seventeen Proven Out-of-Bounds Plays and Last-Second Shots That Will Score Points and the Only Tap Play That You Will Ever Need

This chapter includes seventeen out-of-bounds plays and last-second shot plays:

- One zone out-of-bounds play with five separate options
- Three side out-of-bounds plays with a game winning option
- Eleven out-of of-bounds (under the basket) plays
- Two last-second shot plays with multiple options

When I was coaching, I would select three under-the-basket plays and two side-in plays. I would only use one zone out-of-bounds play with five different options. Then, I would keep the others in reserve to be used the second time we played the same team or in key situations.

Zone Out-of-Bounds

- Inbounder 4 hits the ball as 2 sprints to the three-point area.
- 5 sprints to the opposite low post.
- 3 hits the gap for a possible layup (fig. 6.1).
- 4 can pass to 3, or to 5 inside, or to 2 in the three-point area.

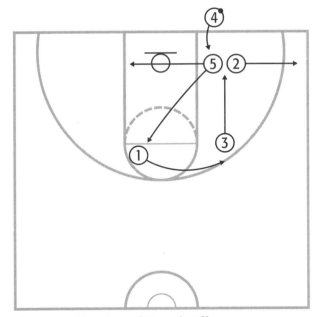

Figure 6.1 Zone Out-of-Bounds Offense

- If 3 is not open, he flashes to the opposite foul-line elbow as 1 replaces in the three-point area.
- 4 can pass to 1.
- 1 looks to pass to 3 at elbow for jump shot.
- 4 steps inbounds for pass from 3 for easy layup.

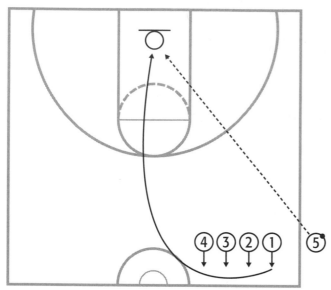

Figure 6.2 Line In Side Out-of-Bounds

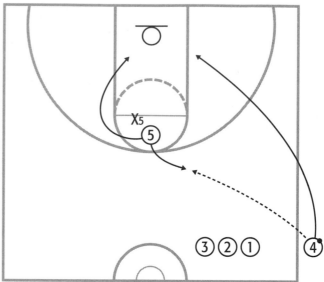

Figure 6.4 Game-Winner Option

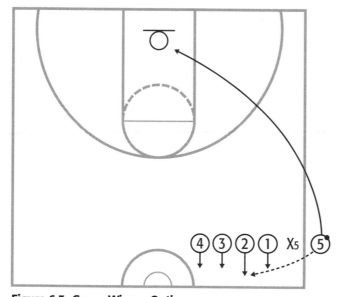

Figure 6.3 Game-Winner Option

Line In Side Out-of-Bounds

- 5 takes the ball out.
- Inbounder calls number (1, 2, 3, or 4), and player sprints to basket (fig. 6.2).
- If pass is not made to sprinting 1 player, 2 flashes back for pass from inbounder.
- This can be used as a setup play for the game winner in Figure 6.3.

Game-Winner Options

- Inbounder will fake once or twice toward midcourt to bring defender to his right, while he throws a backpass to 2.
- Inbounder then races to the hoop and catches the return pass from 2 for the layup (fig. 6.3).
- If teams make an adjustment by putting a player back, we will then put our 5 player back.
- 5 flashes to receive the ball from the inbounder.
- Inbounder cuts to hoop and gets the return pass from 5 (fig. 6.4).
- You will have a two-on-one situation as 5 cuts to the basket.

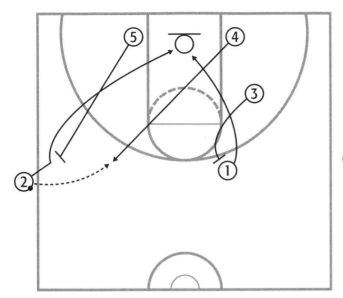

Figure 6.5 Side Out-of-Bounds

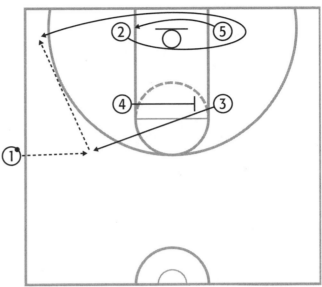

Figure 6.6 Side Out-of-Bounds for Three-Pointer

Side Out-of-Bounds (fig. 6.5)

- 2 passes to 4.
- 5 sets a pick for 2 as 3 sets a pick for 1.
- 4 looks for 1 cutting first.
- If 1 does not receive pass from 4, he clears out, or 4 looks for inbounder cutting off 5 pick after one-second pause.

Side Out-of-Bounds for Three-Pointer (fig. 6.6)

- Your best three-point shooter should be in the 2 position.
- 2 and 5 exchange positions.
- 4 sets a pick for 3.
- 1 passes to 3 and then sprints to set up double pick for 2.
- 2 hesitates until both 1 and 5 have set up the double pick.
- He then flashes to three-point area for pass from 3 and three-point attempt.

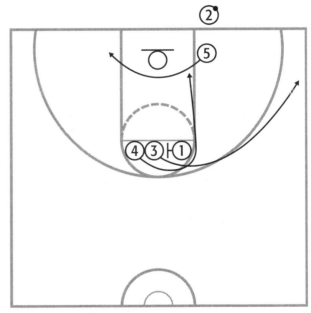

Figure 6.7 Against Man-to-Man

Against Man-to-Man

- 1 sets pick for 3 and 4.
- 3 cuts to three-point area.
- 4 cuts to basket.
- 5 cuts to weak side (fig. 6.7).

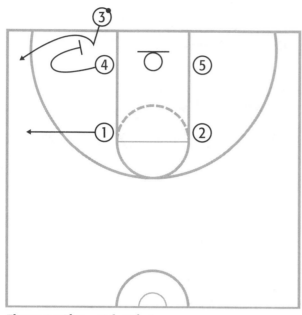

Figure 6.8 Three-Point Shot

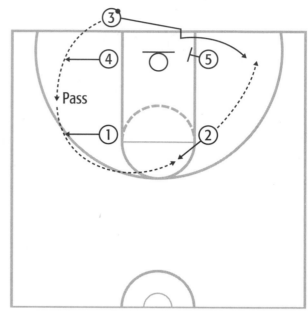

Figure 6.9 Three-Point Play Man-to-Man or Zone

Three-Point Shot

- 3 takes the ball out.
- 4 flashes to corner for pass from 3.
- 4 passes to 1, cutting wide.
- 4 sets pick for 3.
- 3 cuts to three-point area for pass from 1 and a three-point attempt (fig. 6.8).

Three-Point Play Man-to-Man or Zone

- 3 takes the ball out.
- 4 flashes wide with 1.
- 3 passes to 4.
- 5 sets pick for 3.
- 2 passes to 3 for weak-side three-point attempt (fig. 6.9).

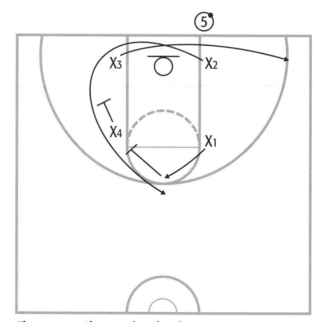

Figure 6.10 Three-Point Shot by X2

- 5 takes the ball out.
- 3 flashes to opposite three-point area.
- 2 flashes off 1 and 4 pick for a three-point attempt (fig. 6.10).

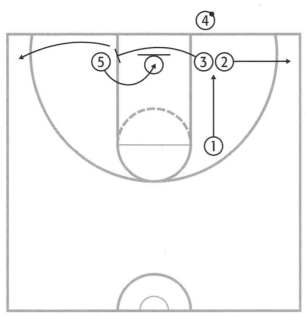

Figure 6.11 Against Man-to-Man or Zone

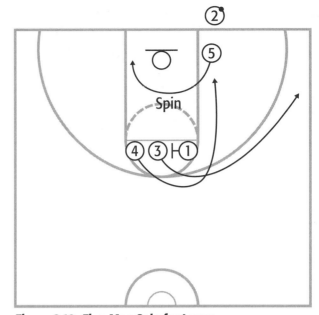

Figure 6.12 Five-Man Spin for Layup

- 4 takes the ball out under the basket.
- 3 sets pick for 5 and then flashes to three-point area.
- 2 flashes to three-point area.
- 4 can pass to 3 or 2 for three-point shot or to 5 for layup (fig. 6.11).

- 2 takes the ball out.
- 5 reaches toward inbounder and then quickly spins to right for potential layup.
- 1 sets pick for 3 and 4.
- 4 cuts up the middle, while 3 flashes to the three-point area.
- 2 passes to 1 on high post, and 1 looks for 2 flashing to three-point area (fig. 6.12).

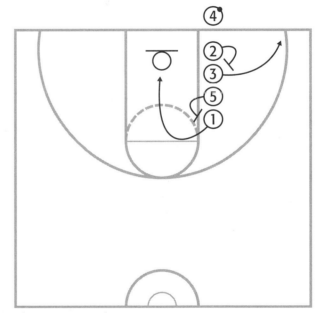

Figure 6.13 Against Man-to-Man

- 4 takes ball out.
- 2 sets a pick for 3.
- 3 can take a short jumper or flash to three-point area.
- 5 sets a pick for 1.
- 1 flashes to the basket (fig. 6.13).

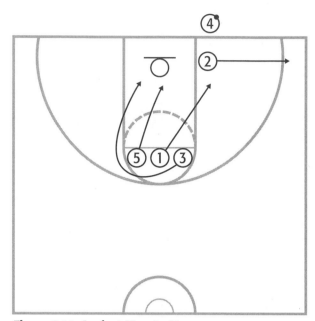

Figure 6.14 Against Man-to-Man

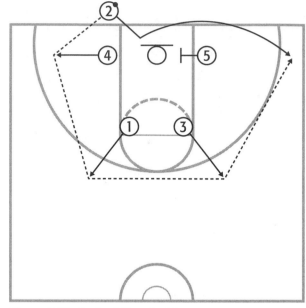

Figure 6.15 Against Man-to-Man

- 4 takes the ball out.
- 2 flashes to three-point area.
- 5 and 1 look for ball as 3 uses 5 and 1 as a blind screen and flashes to basket for layup.
- 4 looks for 3, unless 1 or 5 is open for a score (fig. 6.14).

- 2 takes the ball out.
- 2 passes to 4 and hesitates.
- 4 passes to 1.
- 1 passes to 3.
- 5 sets pick for 2.
- 2 cuts off 5 pick to corner and gets pass from 3 for possible three-point attempt (fig. 6.15).

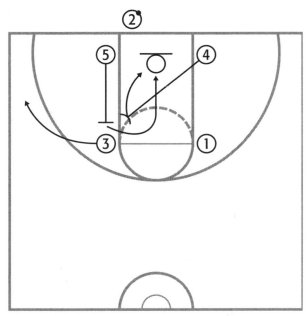

Figure 6.16 Against Man-to-Man

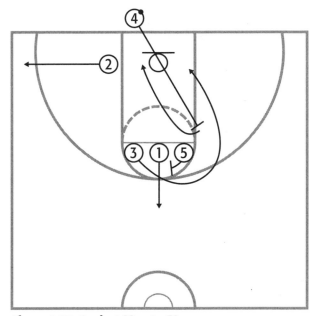

Figure 6.17 Against Man-to-Man

Layups

- 2 takes the ball out.
- 5 sets pick for 3.
- 3 cuts to three-point area.
- 4 picks for 5, as 5 cuts to hoop.
- 4 then cuts to hoop for layup (fig. 6.16).

- 4 takes the ball out.
- 2 flashes to three-point area.
- 4 sets foul line pick for 3.
- 4 flashes to opposite low-post area for possible layup.
- 3 flashes off pick from 5 and 4 and cuts to basket.
- 4 passes to 2.
- 2 looks for cutters 3 or 4 for a possible three-point attempt (fig. 6.17).

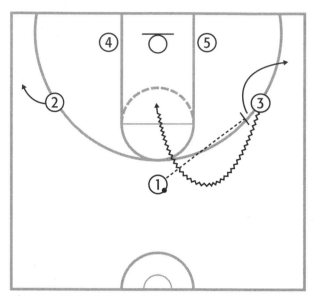

Figure 6.18 Last-Second Shot

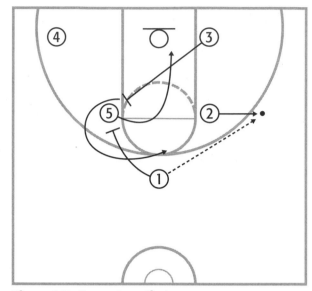

Figure 6.19 Percentage Shot

Last-Second Shot (half-court setup)

- 1 passes to 3.
- 1 sets a pick for 3 and then flashes to the three-point area.
- 3 dribbles off pick by 1 and looks to:
    1. Drive to the basket.
    2. Drive to the basket and pass under to 4 or 5.
    3. Drive to the basket for pull-up jump shot.
    4. Drive to the basket and pass ball to 2 or 1 for three-point shot (fig. 6.18).

Coach's Note: Seventy-five percent of the time, the defender on 2 will leave him open and attempt to double-play the dribbler.

This play is designed to give your team either a low-post or a three-point shot.

- Put your best post player in the 5 spot and your best three-point shooter in the 3 spot.
- 1 passes to 2 at foul line extended.
- 3 sets pick for 5 as 4 clears out.
- After passing to 2, 1 sets pick for 3.
- 3 flashes off 1 pick to three-point area.
- 2 can pass to 5 in low post or to 3 for three-point attempt (fig. 6.19).

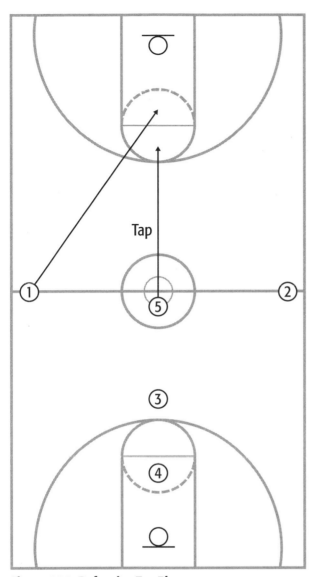

Figure 6.20 Defensive Tap Play

Defensive Tap Play

- 5 taps ball back to 3 or 4, or
- 5 taps to 1 cutting to the basket (fig. 6.20).

Coach's Note: 3 and 4 will prevent an easy layup by your opponent. If 1 is faster than his defender, 1 yells "12" for 12 o'clock and 5 will tap to the foul line area, where 1 will sprint and retrieve the ball for a layup. If 5 yells "6," he will tap to 3 or 4.

Establishing an Offensive System and Identity

Installing an Offensive Package and Developing Unique Play-Calling Skills That Will Keep Defenses Off Guard

In the earlier days of my coaching career, I found it difficult at times to have the right player shooting the ball at the right time, especially at pivotal points in the game. As I thought about it, I decided that I needed to have better control of who shoots the ball and, more important, when he shoots the ball.

I developed a system of three patterned offenses with a numbering system. In this system, I could call out the offensive pattern and put the ball into the hands of our "hot shooter" to put one home in the clutch. Or maybe I wanted the ball in the hands of my point guard, who was, by nature, the one who could penetrate the defense and get to the foul line. Or, if I wanted the low-post player to get the ball to get his man into foul trouble, I would call out his number and get the ball to him.

The following is an example of our numbering system. The system consists of three series and is easy to learn. The point guard will call out two numbers—the first being the number of the series and the second referring to who is getting the ball There are a couple of premises we follow with the three offensive series we run: The point guard either calls the series number first and the play number second. For example, "11" or "12" is a specified play. The only exception is the number "9." If "9" is anywhere in the call, it means a backdoor cut. If the point guard raises his hand and forms a fist, this is another signal to cut backdoor. Any backdoor cut is mandated by a "two-step rule," which means that if the player takes two steps toward the hoop, he must continue to cut backdoor. This has helped us prevent backdoor turnovers.

Series One: Our Basic Pattern

"11" one series for the point-man option (#1)
"12" one series for the guard (#2)
"13" one series for the small forward (#3)
"14" one series for the power forward (#4)
"15" one series for the center (#5)
"19" "9" always means cut backdoor

Series Two: Our Basic Pattern

"21" two series with point guard driving for layup
"22" two series with 2 crisscrossing with 3
"23" two series with 3 crisscrossing with 2
"24" two series with pass to 4
"25" two series with pass to 5
"29" "9" means cut backdoor

Series Three: Our Basic Pattern

"32" three series for 2 (give and go)
"33" three series for 3 backdoor or drive
"34" three series for 4
"35" three series for 5
"39" "9" means cut backdoor

In this system, if the point guard calls just the series number 1 through 3, the team runs the basic pattern. If he calls a series number followed by another number, this is the player the ball goes to. For example, using the number 15, the 1 is the series, and the ball goes to 5, the center. If the number is 24, the series is 2, and the ball goes to our 4 player, the power forward.

Three golden rules on all three offenses follow:

1. If the point guard calls a series followed by the number "9"—for example, "19-29-39"— the player is closely guarded and should cut backdoor.
2. If the point guard raises his hand and forms a fist, it is another signal to cut backdoor.
3. To prevent the guard from turning the ball over because the offensive player faked but did not cut backdoor, we installed the two-step rule. If a player takes two steps toward the hoop, he must cut backdoor. This rule helped us prevent backdoor turnovers.

The series options follow:

1. Point guard can drive for a layup.
2. Pick and roll by the center for a layup.
3. High-percentage jump shot by the 2-guard.
4. Three-point shot for 3 behind a double screen.
5. Low-post one-on-one play for either 4 or 5.

Series 1: Our Basic Pattern

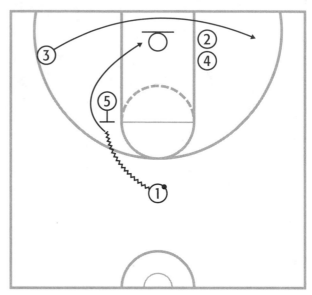

Figure 7.1 Layup or Pick and Roll

Layup or Pick and Roll

- 3 cuts to weak side.
- 1 dribbles off 5 pick for layup, and 3 and 4 drop back on defense (fig. 7.1).

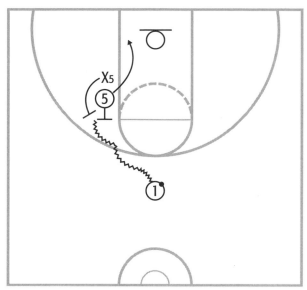

Figure 7.2 Pick and Roll ("11")

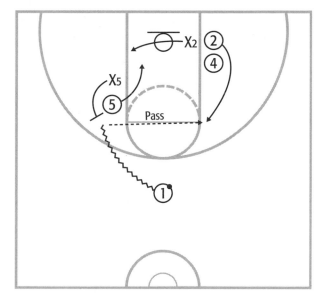

Figure 7.3 Two-Guard Shot ("12")

"11"

- If 5 defender jumps out to stop 1, 5 rolls opposite defender and follows foul line so point can bounce pass to him for layup.
- If 5 follows the foul line, the point guard will know where he is.
- Point must stop at the foul line extended (fig. 7.2).

"12"

- If on the pick and roll, X2 defender sags and picks up 5 rolling to the basket.
- 2 flashes to the elbow for a pass from 1 (foul line extended) and shot (fig. 7.3).

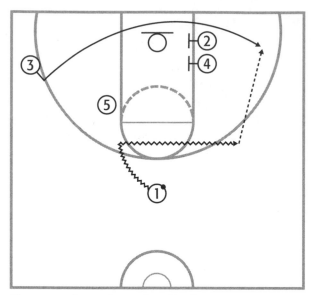

Figure 7.4 Three-Player Shot ("13")

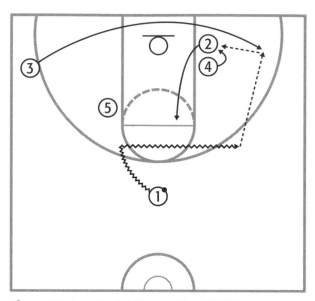

Figure 7.5 Low-Post 4 One-on-One ("14")

"13"

- 1 starts to dribble toward 3 looking first for backdoor cut by 3.
- 3 must step toward 1 before starting his backdoor cut.
- If no backdoor layup, 3 continues to cut behind 2, and 4 twin picks for shot (fig. 7.4).
- 1 dribbles to right and passes to 3.

"14"

- 3 cuts to weak side and receives pass from 1.
- 2 flashes to high post.
- 4 posts low for pass from 3 and one-on-one (fig. 7.5).

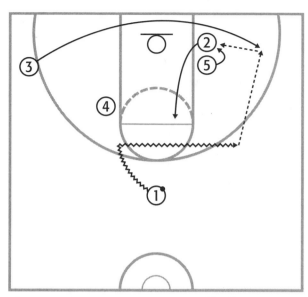

Figure 7.6 Low-Post 5 One-on-One ("15")

"15"

• Same as "14," except for 5 player (fig. 7.6).

Series 2: Our Basic Pattern

Series Two is our double-stack offense, which was originally used by Coach John Thompson at Georgetown University many years ago. I added a number of different options to make it now more of a coach-controlled set. The basic pattern will give you a guard driving for a layup or a pick and roll with the high-post player. Your 1, 2, and 3 guards will get a three-point attempt from the top of the key if their defensive players attempt to help prevent the drive to the basket or pick and roll. Other options include post players and backdoor cuts. They are as follows:

"21" Point guard driving for layup
"22" 2 crisscrosses with 3 for score
"23" 3 crisscrosses with 2 for score
"24" 4-post score
"25" 5-post score
"29" backdoor cut

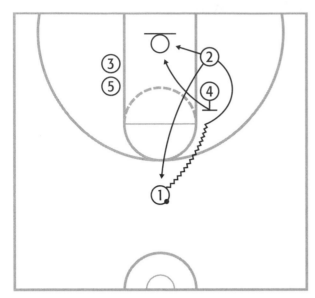

Figure 7.7 Basic Pattern ("21")

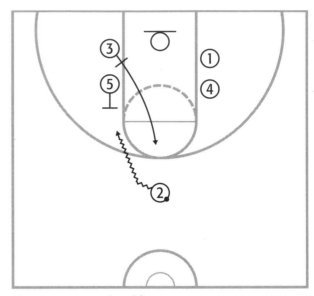

Figure 7.8 Opposite Side

"21"

- 1 dribbles either right or left.
- As 1 picks a direction, 2 flashes to three-point area.
- 4 sets pick and roll.
- If 1 is stopped at foul line extended, he first looks for 4 rolling to the basket, then to 2 at the three-point area for an open shot (fig. 7.7).

Opposite Side

- 2 must now dribble opposite 1, as 3 flashes to point.
- 2 dribbles to basket after pick by 5, or 2 stops at foul line extended and looks for 5 rolling to basket or pass to 3 for three-point shot. (fig. 7.8).

Coach's Note: If 2 stops at foul line and passes to 3 at the point, 2 takes 3 spot in the stack.

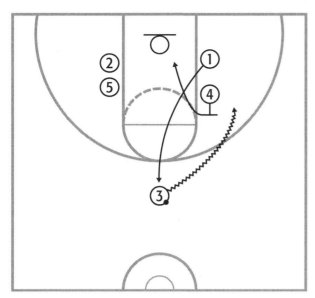

Figure 7.9 At the Point

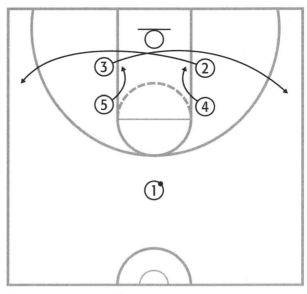

Figure 7.10 "22" and "23"

At the Point

- 3 dribbles to the right and stops at foul line extended and passes to 4, rolling to the basket, or back to 1 at the point for a three-point shot (fig. 7.9).

"22" and "23"

- 22 and 23 is a crisscross with 2 and 3, and the point guard looking to pass to the better shooter.
- As 2 and 3 crisscross, 4 and 5 flash to low-post position (fig. 7.10).
- If 2 or 3 have no shot, they look to pass into the low post for 4 or 5.
- If no shot is available, the ball is passed back out to the point.

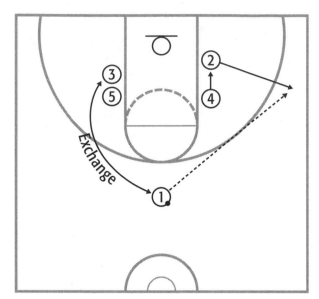

Figure 7.11 "24"

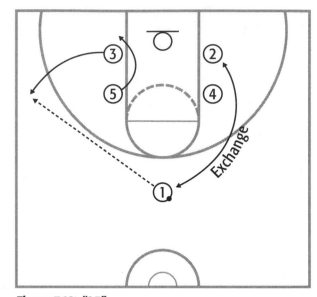

Figure 7.12 "25"

"24"

- 2 pops out for pass from 1.
- 4 posts low.
- 3 pops out and exchanges with 1 to prevent defensive help (fig. 7.11).
- 2 passes to 4.

"25"

- Same as "24," except ball is passed to 5.
- 1 and 2 exchange (fig. 7.12).
- 3 passes to 5.

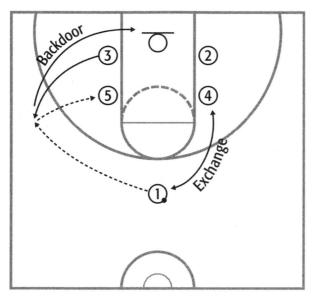

Figure 7.13 "29"

Series 3: Our Basic Pattern

Series Three started out primarily as a stall offense, looking only for the backdoor cut to the wingmen or the give and go from the point position. It is mainly used in the last four minutes of the game. We added a couple of options to the basic offense:

"31" point guard drives to the basket.
"32" give and go.
"33" backdoor cut from the weak side.
"34/35" low-post one-on-one play.
"39" backdoor cut from weak side.

"31"

- 1 passes to either wing.
- If 1 passes to 2, 5 sets pick for 1 for layup.
- If 2 does not pass to 1, 4 pops out to point and gets pass from 2 (fig. 7.14).
- 1 replaces 4.

"29"

- Can be run from either side.
- 3 pops out.
- 1 passes to 3.
- 4 and 1 exchange to prevent defensive help.
- 3 passes to 5 at high post and cuts backdoor to get pass from 5 (fig. 7.13).

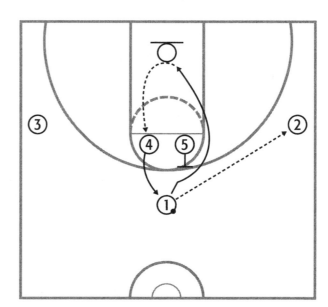

Figure 7.14 "31"

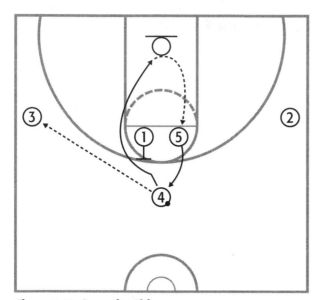

Figure 7.15 Opposite Side

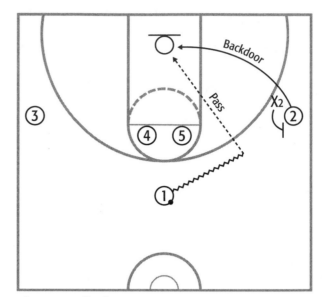

Figure 7.16 "39"

Opposite Side

- 4 passes to 3.
- 4 cuts off pick from 1 and gets pass from 3.
- 5 pops out to point and gets pass from 3 (fig. 7.15).
- 4 replaces 5 on foul line.

Coach's Note: This offense can be run over until the defense tries to deny the pass to the wings.

"39"

- 1 calls "39" and dribbles to set up easy backdoor pass.
- 2 takes step toward 1 to bring his defensive man high and then cuts backdoor (fig. 7.16).

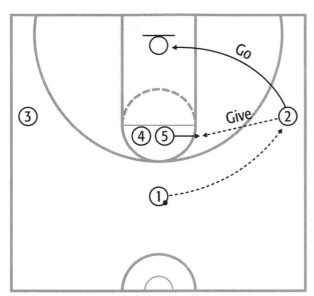

Figure 7.17 Give and Go "32"

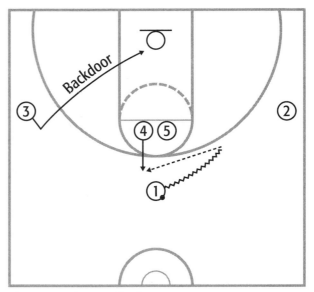

Figure 7.18 "33" or "39"

"32"

- 1 passes to 2.
- 5 flashes to elbow and pass from 2.
- 2 passes to 5 and cuts to basket and give-and-go pass from 5 (fig. 7.17).

"33" or "39"

- 1 calls "33" and dribbles toward 2.
- 4 pops out for pass from 1.
- 4 passes to 3 for one-on-one play. If 3 is guarded, he calls "39" and cuts backdoor (fig. 7.18).

"34"/"35"

- 1 passes to 2.
- 1 and 3 exchange.
- 5 flashes to low post and pass from 2 for post one-on-one (fig. 7.19).

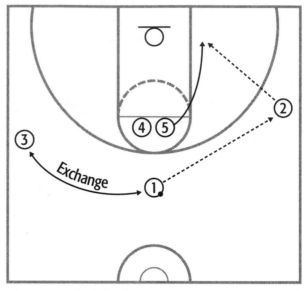

Figure 7.19 "34"/"35"

Defense Wins Championships

Defensive Philosophies That Turn Average Players into Excellent Defenders

Before the start of each season, it is the coach's responsibility to evaluate his players' talents. Every season brings new faces, so you really never know what you're working with until you have run the first couple practices, when you see who can run, who can jump, who can box out, and, most important, who can hustle. I say "most important" because hustle is the one facet of basketball that can bring you the greatest success as a coach. You win possessions on hustle, you win games on hustle, you win championships on hustle, and you build a reputation for your program on hustle. Yet, unfortunately, it is something you can't teach. If that were the case, I probably would have designated an entire chapter on "coaching hustle" alone; it was that important to our teams' success year after year. If you're lucky enough to have five guys on the court who want to win every time, as I did for most of my career, you'd understand what a little hustle can do for you.

If it is true that offense wins football games and defense wins championships, the same could be said about basketball. If you look at the perennial successful programs in the college game—teams like Duke, Kansas, Maryland, and Kentucky—you will see they all pride themselves on playing solid fundamental defense. These teams don't just play on one end of the court like some professional organizations do; they win with their defense. One of my professional idols, Bobby Knight, would spend entire practices coaching defense, without even bringing a basketball onto the court. Instead, he would concentrate on defensive slides, footwork, and one-on-one matchup defense. In essence, he was teaching his players hustle, and it was that grit-before-glory approach that won him eleven Big Ten titles and three national championships. As a coach, I tried to emulate this approach.

In terms of defensive schemes, some coaches make the mistake of committing to one type of defense—either a zone or man. They say, "We are too slow to play man-to-man, so we will play zone," or "We are too small to play zone, so we have to match up man-to-man." Either way, to succeed, you need to have an element of variety when you're playing defense. You have to change things and give your opponent as many different looks as possible. I know because I made the same mistake in the beginning of my coaching career that young coaches make today.

I was a zone-defensive coach. It was what I was raised on during my playing days. We hardly ever played man-to-man defense, and it was what I knew best, so I went with it. We played the 2-1-2, 3-2, 1-2-2, 1-3-1, the box and one, and the triangle and two defenses. I would mix and match each of these defenses to confuse the other coaches. Yet I realized that the only coaches I was confusing were the younger ones. The experienced coaches knew how to attack a zone, no matter which one I was in, so I had a hard time beating their teams.

A few years later, I heard another coach say something that changed my mind about defense. At a county tournament seeding meeting, I overheard one of the coaches in my league saying something to the effect that "St. Mary's is a great offensive team with some good shooters. Just imagine how tough they would be if their defense was just as good."

Later on in that season, we played in the sectional state finals. Our team was big up front—6'5", 6'4", and 6'4"—and we started in our 2-1-2 zone. Our opponent was a little smaller and quickly jumped out to a 4-0 lead and then held the ball! We stayed in our zone and they continued to hold the ball. At the end of the first quarter, the score was still actually 4–0 in their favor. There was no shot clock at the high school level back then, so you got away with doing those things. So we had no choice but to change to a man-to-man defense and, because of our inexperience with this, they beat us. Basketball history will show that many zone-defensive teams will lose with four minutes to go when their opponent would hold the ball and make them play man-to-man.

It was then I realized that an abundance of points could give you only so much. If you didn't have the defense to stop a team, you would be in trouble. The very next season, and for the rest of my coaching career, we were a man-to-man defensive team. I sent for every book and video I could find on man-to-man defense, and I did what every coach would do—learn. Although there were times where we switched to a zone or box and one, we stayed primarily in a man-on-man scheme. I even refused to allow my freshmen or junior varsity coaches to play zone defense, so the players would have a solid background on defense when they were ready to move up to the varsity team. Our players were never lazy, and making them play man-to-man helped assure them that they had "hustle."

Today I'm a pressure-defense convert. My philosophy is to make the opponent's offense make plays to beat us. As a coach, I'll match up my guys with anyone on the court because, above all else, I know that even though I might not have the quickest, strongest, or most talented players, my players are willing to hustle all game, and I use that to my team's advantage.

Essential Defensive Fundamentals
That Must Be Mastered

- Always play half of the offensive player's strong side.
- Force the opponent away from his intended path or his strong side.
- Never give up the baseline.
- Use defensive rotation.
- Never be more than one arm's length away from the offensive player.
- If the offensive player picks up his dribble, yell "Trap," and stay within six inches of your man.
- When smothering your defender, yell "Deny" to let teammates know they have to deny their men.
- Prevent the fast break by tying up the rebounder.
- Always look to double-up your man.
- Don't reach in and foul.
- Prevent giving one-on-one or "bonus" fouls in each half.
- Always meet the ball if your offensive player doesn't.
- If your offensive man is one pass away from the player, deny the pass.
- On backdoor cuts, open to the ball.
- Never leave your feet in the post area unless your opponent is in the air.
- On backdoor cuts, obstruct your player's vision.
- Always box out.
- Look to draw charges.
- Talk on defense.
- Always pick up loose ball out of bounds.

I've learned that there are five main reasons for playing man-to-man pressure defense, and they all account for more wins:

1. You will score more points.
2. The pressing team will always outlast a team in poor shape.
3. It disrupts the play pattern of the offense, and they have to scramble to beat you.

4. During the season, especially early on, teams are not ready to handle the press.

5. It prevents a four-corner delay game by opponents, which usually hold up the entire contest.

Principles of Man-to-Man Pressure

Defensive Positioning

Your defensive position as a stationary player must be one hand tracing or shadowing the ball, with the other hand up to prevent an easy pass.

- Players always play one arm's length away, in case of a loose ball or to be able to get in a passing lane.
- The rule of thumb is for a player to stay about three feet from an opponent, and never more.
- When dribbling, have your palm up to the opponent's strong side, either right or left, and force him away from his intended path.
- When the opponent picks up his dribble, play within six inches of him, smothering him. Make him make a play!
- If the offensive player tends to shoot straight up, the defender should front him, raising one hand to block his vision without reaching in and committing a foul.
- Come down and box out after every shot.

Guarding the Man with the Ball

- Harass.
- Defenders should keep their backs straight, hips low, and feet shoulder-width apart.
- Keep one hand higher than ball, lower hand palm out.
- Stay close enough to touch player.
- Overplay his strong side.
- Step and slide-step in desired direction and slide trailing foot.

- Step-step method: attack player, retreat when player makes offensive move toward basket, and then move laterally to prevent penetration.
- Be active and aggressive.
- When your man stops his dribble, grow tall, tighten up, and make him lob the ball over your hands.
- Front a good shooter.
- When a shot is taken, go directly for a rebound and box out their best rebounder.

Guarding the Post Man

- Always play in front of the man in a low-post area.
- At the foul line, play him to his strong side and straddle post man's inside leg. This way, the defensive player's arm nearest to the ball is up and blocking the post man's vision.
- Beat the man across the lane.

Fronting the Post Man

- Disallow any pass to him.
- Expect help on lob pass.
- Call for help.
- Put your elbow on his chest and your foot between his legs; this way you can feel where he is going and still be able to watch the ball.
- Don't allow him to cut.
- Wheel inside and box him out on the outside shot.

Denying Position

If your man does not have the ball, you must be in a denying position. You must be able to see the man and the ball at the same time.

- The denying position means having one hand in the passing lane at all times.
- Account for the threat of a pass by knowing where an opposing player has a tendency to pass the ball.

- The player who is smothering his player will always yell "Deny" to his teammates. It lets them know that their man is cornered and that, once he picks up his dribble, he's trapped.

Playing Against Cutting and Screening

- Make the cutter or dribbler go wide and allow your teammate to slide through.
- If your man is cutting off an offside screen, beat him to the ball.
- If the team you're playing uses shuffles or extreme numbers of cuts, anticipate them and draw charges.
- If you must "switch," the screener's man should take the ball.
- If the offensive players split the post, get close to the post man and force your player wide.
- If guards and forward exchange places, the defenders should switch.
- Always help one on one.
- Double-up from blind side on overdribbler.
- Talk on cuts and screens. Communicate.

Switch Calls

Sometimes when your team is playing a man-to-man defense and the opponent sets a screen for your man, it is necessary to call a "switch" with your teammate, telling him that you will now cover his man and he will guard the player you've been guarding. Players would often call "Switch" and the flip would not occur, resulting in an easy shot or basket. We have eliminated this problem by saying, "We will always switch" on a pick. Although this may create some matchup problems for us, our philosophy is that it is better to play sound defense than to have teams set picks and work backdoor cuts on us all day long.

Rotate on Baseline Drives

On any baseline drives, all coaches should instruct their players not to allow them, but there are still many times in a game where the defender will allow his man to work the baseline for a score. The baseline should be used as a defender, meaning a player can position himself to trap his opponent if he chooses to go baseline. With this in mind, we try to teach our players about defensive rotation with weak-side help on the baseline. According to this principle, you always have help to the weak side if you need it.

Guard-Center Double-Up

This tactic pertains to guarding the offensive post-up when the ball is sent down into the low-post for a center or power forward. Many teams will have the guard nearest the ball side "sag" back and double-up on the post player when he has the ball. This is a common tactic that we usually see in the professional game. When a powerful, dominating center like Shaquille O'Neal or Hakeem Olajuwon gets the ball in the paint, a guard is the first one to come for help, which may sometimes result in a kick-out for a perimeter shot and a score, especially at that level of play. This is an acceptable way of stopping that player, but we teach our sagging guards that if they are going to double-up on the low post, the first thing to do is take away the dribble. When the opponent attempts to dribble, the defender should get his hand between the floor and the offensive player's hand. Taking away the dribble eliminates half of his offense.

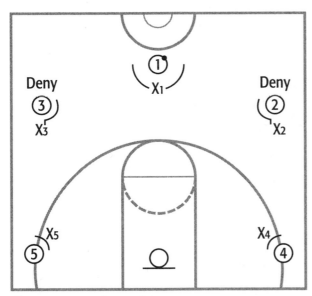

Figure 8.1 Smother and Deny

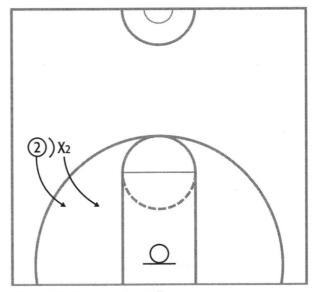

Figure 8.2 Open to the Ball

Man-to-Man Fundamentals

Smother and Deny

- X2 and X3 are within one step in the direction of the ball and then deny with one hand in the passing lane (fig. 8.1).
- X2 and X3 should hit the gap for a steal if their players do not meet the ball.
- If X1 passes to X2, 1 should take one step toward X2 and into a deny position.
- 4 is one pass away, so he will deny.

Open to the Ball

- This is a very important defensive fundamental when you are denying the pass.
- Your man will cut backdoor.
- You must open to the ball by pivoting (fig. 8.2).
- Your pivot is so that your eyes are on the passer for the possible intercept.

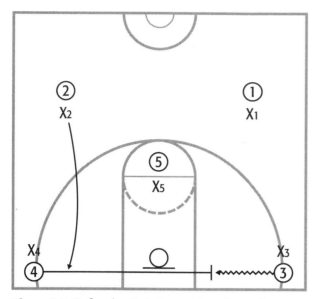

Figure 8.3 Defensive Rotation on Baseline Drive

Figure 8.4 Low-Post Defense

Defensive Rotation

- 3 drives baseline.
- X4 defender flashes to pick up X3.
- X4 looks first to draw a charge, then stops his penetration.
- X2 must rotate down to pick up 4 (fig. 8.3).

Coach's Note: Some coaches teach their center (X5) to pick up the driving 3. Doing this, however, leaves 5 open for an easy shot and can cause X5 to get into foul trouble.

Low-Post Defense

- Always play in front of low-post player.
- On an over-the-top pass, X3 flashes to help and double on 5.
- X1 flashes down to pick up open 3 (fig. 8.4).

This is our basic defensive package and their calls:

Army: Our pressure man-to-man defense.
Navy: Our man-to-man half-court trapping defense.
I-Defense: Zone used to prevent fast breaks, stopping penetration at the top of key.

We divide the court as follows:

100 equals full court.
75 equals three-quarter court.
50 equals half-court.

For example, Army 100 would be our full-court-pressure man-to-man defense, and Navy 100 would be our full-court trapping-zone defense.

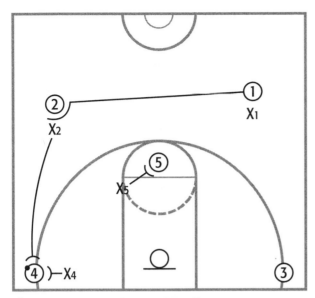

Figure 8.5 Navy 50 Man-to-Man Trap

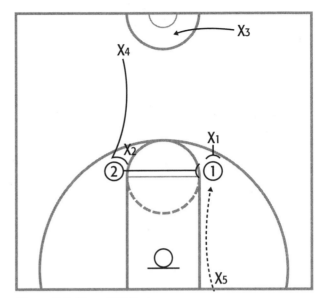

Figure 8.6 Navy 100 Trap

Navy 50 Man-to-Man Trap

- X4 and X2 trap.
- X5 prevents pass to 5.
- X1 prevents pass to 2.
- X3 prevents pass to 3 (fig. 8.5).
- Look for five-second count or intercept passing lanes.

Navy 100 Man-to-Man Trap

- On inbound, pass to 1 or 2.
- X1 and X2 trap 1.
- X5 prevents pass back.
- X4 prevents pass to 2.
- X3 prevents long pass (fig. 8.6).

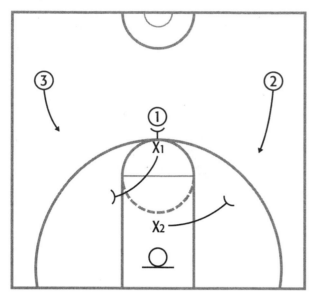

Figure 8.7 "I" Defense (Right)

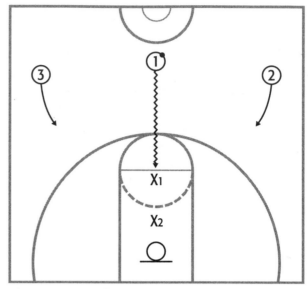

Figure 8.8 "I" Defense (Wrong)

The "I" Defense

- The first two players back on defense will form the "I" defense.
- X1 will position himself at the top of the key.
- X2 is in the paint.
- As the fast break approaches, X1 must fake at 1 and stop the ball at the top of the key (fig. 8.7).
- X2 will then take the first cutter.
- X1 will take 3.

Coach's Note: You must stress that X1 has to position himself at the top of the key and stop the dribbler. If he drops back to the foul-line area, he allows the point guard an easy pull-up jumper from the top of the key (fig. 8.8).

Zone Defenses and Offenses

Utilizing Zone Defenses and Offenses to Stifle Opponents' Tendencies

Sometimes, because of differing athletic abilities, a team does not have the personnel to match up man-to-man defensively against an opponent. In these situations, it makes sense to use some type of zone setup, where you can best utilize the weapons you have. In my coaching career, we always taught the various zones and tried to perfect their execution in practice. After scouting our next opponent, our second team ran the opponent's offense while we worked on our zone defense.

In this chapter, I discuss in great detail what types of zone defenses and offenses are used in basketball. The key to using zones is to use them situationally, which means mixing and matching what you give your opponent, depending on what you are seeing in the game. We used certain zones sparingly and under specific circumstances. For example, on all out-of-bounds plays under the basket, we used a tight 2-1-2 zone. We also used a tight 3-2 zone against a team that had two or more exceptional outside shooters. This gave us help on the perimeter as we guarded these shots. Our 1-3-1 zone was used only when we employed our three-quarter-court 1-3-1 trap. We then fell back into a half-court 1-3-1 trapping zone.

If a team had an exceptional outside shooting guard, we tried our stunting 3-2 zone, then moved right into a hidden box-and-one to try to stop their best man.

Basic Zone Defenses

2-1-2 Zone (see figs. 9.1, 9.2, 9.3)
3-2 Zone (see figs. 9.4, 9.5, 9.6)
3-2 Stunt (see figs. 9.7, 9.8)
1-3-1 Zone (see figs. 9.9, 9.10, 9.11)
1-3-1 Three-Quarter Trap (see figs. 9.12, 9.13, 9.14, 9.15)

2-1-2 ZONE

Keys to Execution

- Always stay within the three-point circle.
- Force the ball to wing opposite their best shooter.
- Always key on their best shooter.

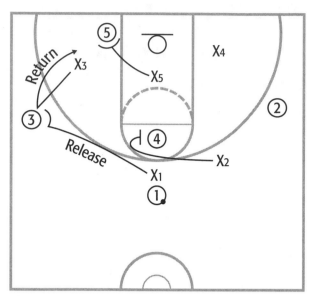

Figure 9.1 2-1-2 Zone Rotation

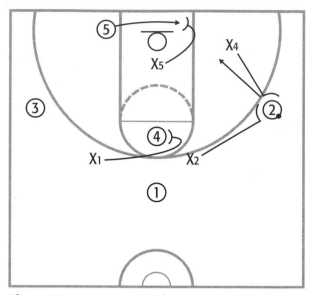

Figure 9.2 2-1-2 Zone Rotation

Rotation

- On pass from 1 to 3, X3 flashes to PU3.
- X1 flashes to O3 and yells "Release."
- X3 returns to his position.
- X2 slides in front of 4 to prevent pass, and then boxes out 4.
- X5 slides to O5 (fig. 9.1).

Rotation

- On crosscourt pass to 2, X4 flashes to O2.
- X2 flashes to O2, yells "Release," and X4 returns under and picks up O5 flashing to strong-side low post.
- X5 Flashes to strong-side low post.
- X1 slides in front of high post 4 (fig. 9.2).

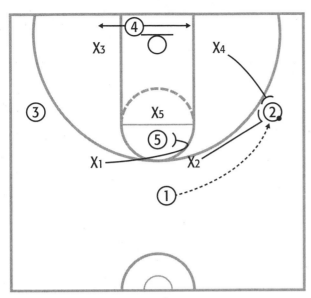

Figure 9.3 2-1-2 Zone Rotation

Rotation

- If the high-post player is their best shooter, X5 plays close behind.
- If the pass is made by 1, X1 and X2 double on 5 and prevent his first dribble.
- On pass to 2, X4 flashes to 2 and calls "Release."
- X4 goes back, X1 plays in front of 5 with X5 behind 5 (fig. 9.3).

3-2 ZONE

Keys to Execution

- The 3-2 zone is effective against teams with good outside shooters.
- The zone should key and cheat in the zone area of their best shooters.
- X2 and X3 should be your best guard rebounders.
- X2 and X3 become rebounders when the ball is on the opposite side.
- Always keep the zone tight.
- Stay within the three-point circle.

Rotation

- X4 takes shooter.
- X5 flashes to strong-side post.
- X2 flashes back to weak side for possible rebound (fig. 9.4).
- Until the ball moves, you are in a 3-2 zone.

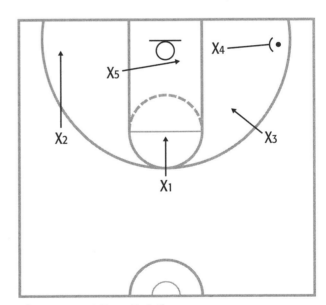

Figure 9.4 3-2 Zone Rotation

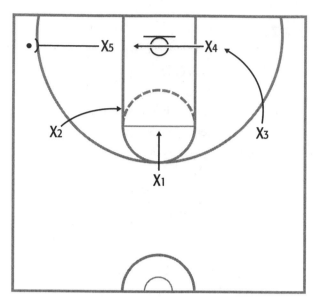

Figure 9.5 3-2 Zone Rotation

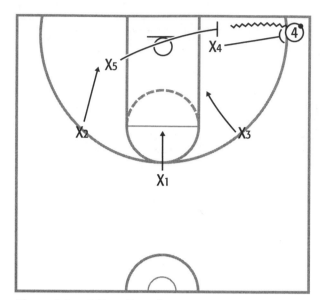

Figure 9.6 3-2 Zone Rotation

Rotation

- Same rotation as in Figure 9.4, but now X3 is the weak-side rebounder (fig. 9.5).

Rotation

- X5 flashes to O4 on baseline drive.
- Look to draw charge first, then contain him.
- X5 should retreat and double on 4.
- X2 drops back for weak-side help (fig. 9.6).

3-2 STUNTING ZONE INTO A BOX-AND-ONE

Rules for Execution

- Normal 3-2 zone should have best guard rebounders in the X1 and X2 positions because they become weak-side rebounders.
- In stunting 3-2 zone, the best rebounder is in the middle (X3).
- Stunting 3-2 has a big advantage: the player defending the high-scoring shooter does not get worn out.

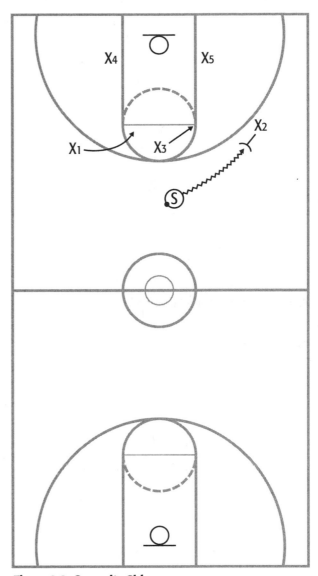

Figure 9.8 Opposite Side

Rotation

- If the shooter is in X1 zone area, X1 plays him man-to-man and the rest of the defenders form the box.
- If the shooter is in X2 zone area, X2 plays him man-to-man and the rest of the defenders form the box (figs. 9.7 and 9.8)

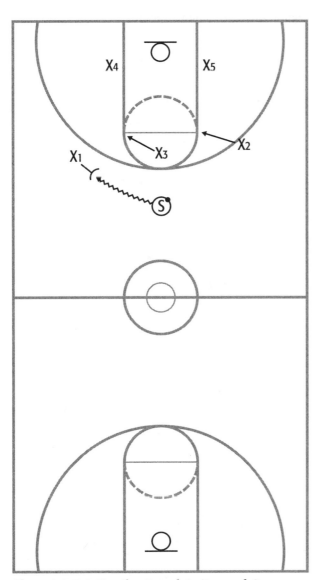

Figure 9.7 3-2 Stunting Zone into Box-and-One

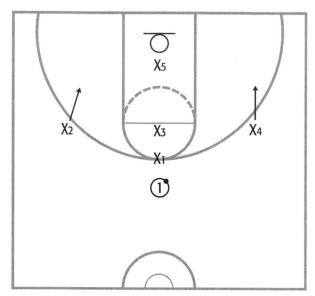

Figure 9.9 1-3-1 Zone Rotation

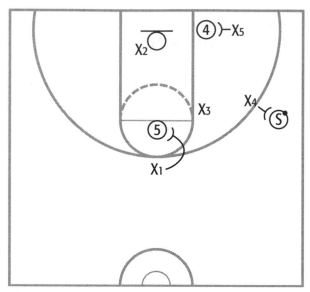

Figure 9.10 1-3-1 Zone Rotation

1-3-1 ZONE

Rotation

- X1 should force pass to wing, opposite the opponent's best shooter.
- X2, X4, and X5 become rebounders on the weak side (fig. 9.9).

Rotation

- X4 has man with the ball.
- X3 and X5 are on the ball side.
- X5 positions himself in front of low-post man.
- X2 should be in position to prevent an over-the-top pass to the low-post player (fig. 9.10).

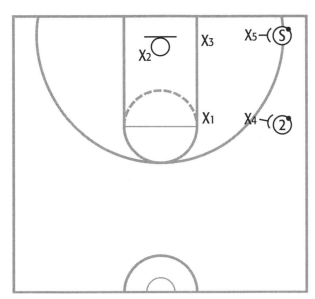

Figure 9.11 1-3-1 Zone Rotation

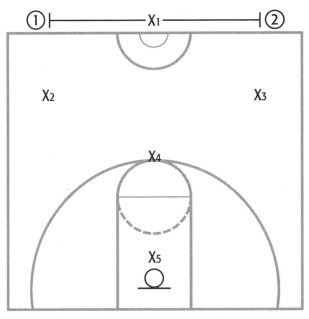

Figure 9.12 1-3-1 Three-Quarter-Court Zone Rotation

Rotation

- X5 takes the man with the ball.
- X3 fronts low-post man.
- X2 prevents an over-the-top pass.
- X1 fronts high-post player (fig. 9.11).

1-3-1 THREE-QUARTER-COURT ZONE TRAP "CANARSIE"

Rotation

- X1 forces the ball to the sides (must keep the ball out of the middle to execute the trap; fig. 9.12).

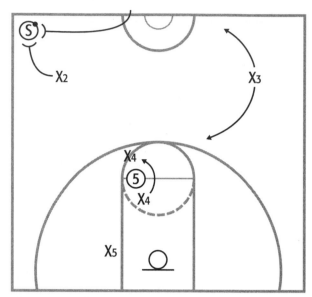

Figure 9.13 First Trap

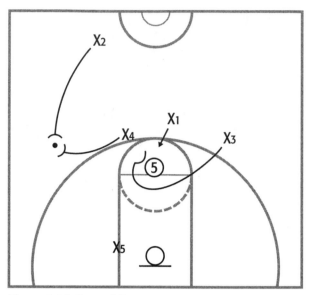

Figure 9.14 Second Trap

Rotation

- X1 and X2 trap when dribbler has one foot over the midcourt line.
- X3 looks for steal as X4 and X5 shift to ball side of the court.
- X4 looks to step in front for steal if the opposition places a man on the high post (fig. 9.13).
- Yell "Dead" as soon as offensive player picks up his dribble, so teammates are aware he can't move.

Rotation

- X2 and X4 trap man on wing.
- X3 flashes behind high-post player and looks to steal pass from wing to high post.
- X1 flashes back to the top of the key (fig. 9.14).

Rotation

- X2 and X5 trap ball in corner.
- X3 must flash from high post and replace X5 to protect inside (fig. 9.15).
- Yell "Dead" as soon as offensive player picks up his dribble, so teammates are aware he can't move.

Coach's Note: The most important slide in the trap is X3 sliding under to protect the basket. If the ball is passed to midcourt, the player should stay in a 1-3-1 half-court zone.

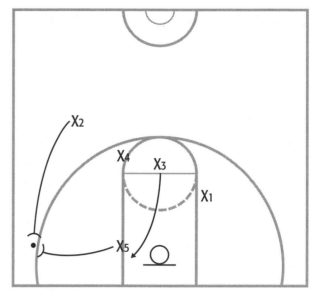

Figure 9.15 Third Trap

1-3-1 OFFENSE AGAINST 2-1-2 ZONE

Changing up our offensive sets frequently caused a lot of confusion for the defense, enough to beat them by fourteen points and win our first state championship. Today, with all the advances and complexities of high school basketball, this is a major reason as to why every team should have at least one or two solid motion offenses that they can run frequently every game. You always need one on the back burner, in case one stalls.

Just as coaches do in every sport, you have to evaluate your personnel to find your strengths and weaknesses before you decide which offense that you want to run. Most coaches will use a 1-3-1 offense against a 2-1-2, 1-2-2, 3-2, or 2-3 zone defense. In fact, many teams will set up their zone and pass the ball to get movement without using some important coaching points that make the 1-3-1 effective. Every zone has a weakness. Just as the 3-2 is open in the three-second area, the 1-3-1 zone is vulnerable in the corners. The key to running the 1-3-1 is to have excellent perimeter shooters who can score from the corners, which was our strength for many years. Because of this, we were able to work this zone offense into our package effectively, and we were quite successful in doing so.

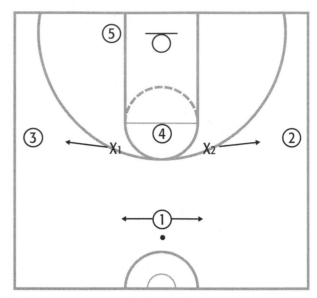

Figure 9.16 Pass to High-Post Player

Pass to High-Post Player

- The point guard must fake a pass to the right and then fake a pass to the left to cause X1 and X2 to step in the direction of his fakes.
- 1 passes to 4 on the high post (fig. 9.16).
- 1 can also now shoot from the top of the key if it is open.

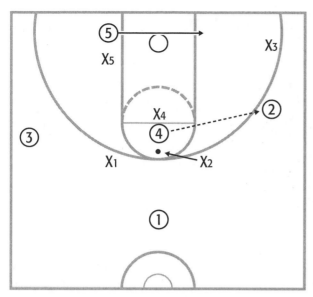

Figure 9.17 Post Player with Ball

Figure 9.18 To Open Player for a Wing Shot

Post Player with the Ball

- High-post player with ball should look for 5 inside.
- Feel which guard is sagging on him and then hit the open man with a pass.
- In this case, X2 is sagging on 4 and 2 is open.
- If 4 passes to 2, 5 must flash to the strong side (fig. 9.17).
- If X3 plays 2 and X4 drops back to pick up 5, 4 is open in the foul-line area.

A Shot from the Wing

- If 1 wants to free 2 for a shot, 1 will dribble directly at X2, then bounce pass to 2.
- If 2 does not have the open shot, 5 will flash to strong-side low-post position to freeze X3, forcing him to play out of position on the post (fig. 9.18).

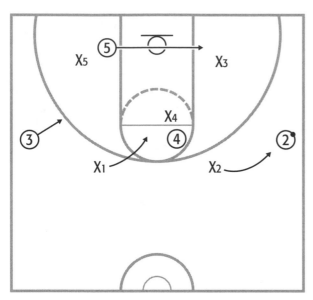

Figure 9.19 Cross-Court Pass

Cross-Court Pass to Opposite Wing Shooter

- When 2 has the ball, the zone will shift to the ball side.
- 3 should stay wide and anticipate a cross-court pass from 2 and a possible a three-point attempt (fig. 9.19).

1-2-2 ZONE MOTION OFFENSE

This type of offense is generally designed to get the ball low and inside to your post players, both the 4-man and the 5-man. It can be used against any type of zone defense, provided your post players touch the ball at least twice before an offensive shot goes up. Because the majority of your shots will come from your front-court players, when a shot goes up it is essential in this setup that at least three players crash the boards for the rebound to get second shots.

The post players start out behind the zone. We call these two the "buddy-buddy" players because they work in conjunction with one another. When the ball goes either high or low, the other post player must curl free in the opposite box or area—the post player with the ball must always look for his "buddy" first. The progression of scoring is simple: When the post player has the ball, he looks for his buddy first. The opposite wing player is the second option, and the other wing player is the third option.

The positioning of the wing players must be at foul line extended, behind the zone defense. They must always be cautious of the skip pass from across the court and rotate up to balance the floor. The key to getting open shots in this setup is the play of the wing players as decoys. They must constantly pass fake and shoot fake with the ball and attack the seam and look inside for the post players. They also have the ability to split two defenders and use a two-handed bounce pass to get the ball in the low post.

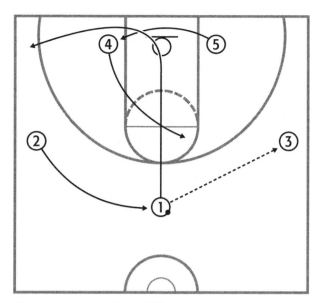

Figure 9.20　1-2-2 Zone Offense

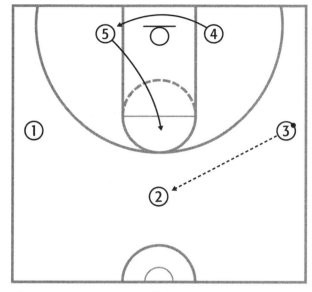

Figure 9.21　1-2-2 Zone Offense

Rotation

- 1 passes to 3.
- 4 flashes to middle-post area.
- 5 replaces 4.
- If 4 has the ball, he looks for 5 at the low post for a one-on-one matchup.
- If 4 draws a double team, he can get the pass out to the wing for a possible shot, or get it back out to the point guard to set up the offense again (fig 9.20).

Rotation

- 3 passes to 2 at the top of the key.
- 2 must hesitate as 5 flashes to the high post at the foul line.
- 5 looks first for his "buddy," 4, then back out to the wings (fig. 9.21).

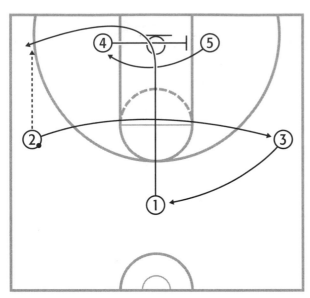

Figure 9.22 Strong-Side Pass

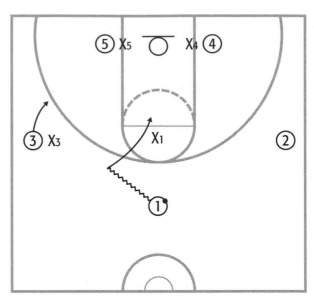

Figure 9.23 Gap Penetration

Strong-Side Pass

- 1 passes to 2.
- 1 then cuts to the same side where he made the pass.
- 2 passes back to 1 in corner.
- 2 cuts to weak-side wing.
- 4 sets pick for 5.
- 1 looks for 5 at the low post for a possible three-point attempt (fig. 9.22).

Gap Penetration

- 1 beats defender one-on-one and drives into lane.
- 1 looks for either 4 or 5 in the low post or 3 shuffling down for a corner jump shot (fig. 9.23).

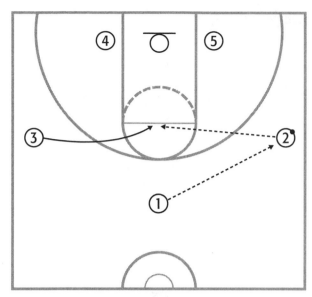

Figure 9.24 Three-Man Inside Offense

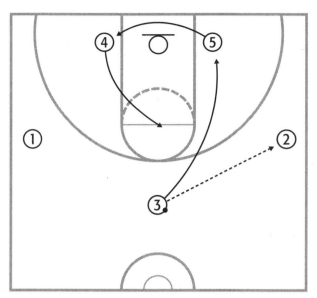

Figure 9.25 Three-Buddy Offense

Three-Man Inside Offense

- 1 passes to 2.
- 3 cuts to foul-line area.
- 3 gets the ball down low to either 4 or 5 or a possible open jump shot (fig. 9.24).

Three-Buddy Offense

- 3 passes to 2.
- 3 cuts to low post.
- 2 passes to either 3, who is cutting into strong-side lane, or 4, who is flashing up to the foul line.
- If 3 gets ball, he looks directly to 5, who is cutting across the lane in the low post.
- If 4 gets ball, he looks for 3, cutting the lane, or 5.
- 2 can also skip pass to 1 on the wing for an open jump shot (fig. 9.25).

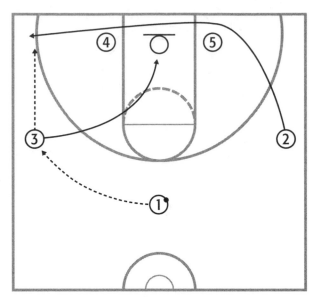

Figure 9.26 Best-Shooter Option

Best-Shooter Option

- 1 passes to 3.
- 2 cuts to strong-side corner and gets pass from 3.
- As 2 shoots jumper from corner, 3 cuts to middle for a possible rebound (fig. 9.26).

STACK OFFENSE

Against a 1-3-1 Defense

- The object is for 1 and 2 to get into the seams between X1, X2, and X3 for a shot at the three-point area.
- The best three-point shooter should play 3.
- 2 should always look to draw X3 out to free up 3 (fig. 9.27).

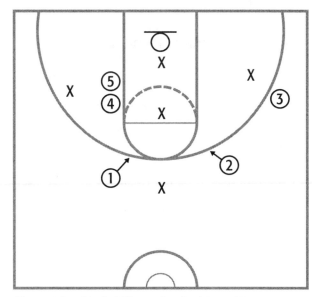

Figure 9.27 Stack Offense Against 1-3-1 Zone

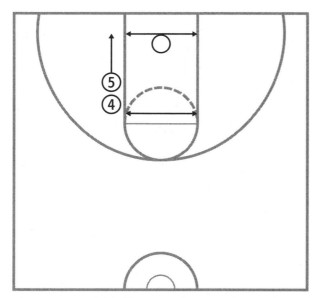

Figure 9.28 Stack Offense Against 4 and 5 Inside

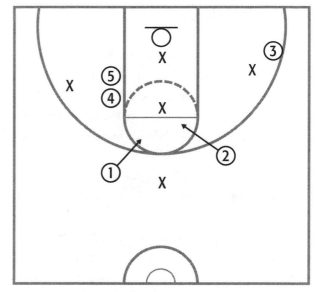

Figure 9.29 Over the Top by 3 or 2

4 and 5 Inside

- 4 is free to flash from foul line, always looking for 5 inside or 3 at the wing.
- 5 looks for an open area down low (fig. 9.28).

Over the Top by 3 or 2

- When 3 has the ball, he looks to either shoot, pass to 4 flashing to strong side, or pass to 5 over the top.
- It 3 passes back to 2, he must look to 5 on weak-side under (fig. 9.29).
- Ball movement is essential.

BOX-AND-ONE OFFENSE

In 1984, my team was ranked seventh in an eight-team conference. More than 90 percent of the teams that played us used a box-and-one defense on our 5' 11" shooting guard. They would have their best defensive player locked man-to-man with him, following him wherever he went. The other four defenders played each box in the paint. Although it was hard to get the ball to this player, we realized that we had to find a way to get him some shots. Our coaching staff came up with a unique offense that was designed to get him the ball at critical spots outside the perimeter. That season, we won the conference championship, and our shooting guard averaged thirty points a game using this box-and-one offense. We installed five separate options off this one set.

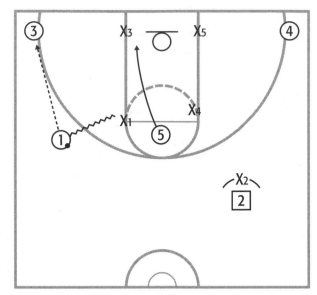

Figure 9.30 Box-and-One Offense, Option 1

Option 1

- Point guard dribbles at X1 at the three-point area, causing him to come out and play him.
- If X1 refuses to come out, 1 has an open three-point shot.
- If X1 comes out to defend, 1 passes the ball to 3, who will have an open shot if X3 refuses to come out and defend him.
- If X3 comes out to defend, 3 hits 5 down low for the easy basket (fig. 9.30).

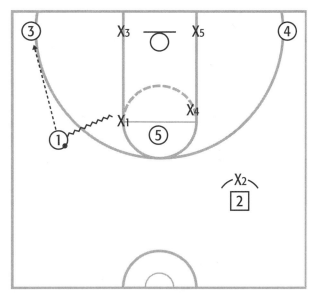

Figure 9.31 Box-and-One Offense, Option 2

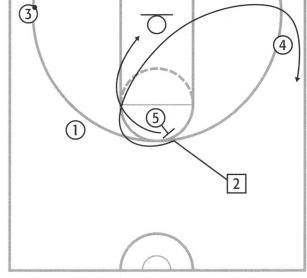

Figure 9.32 Box-and-One Offense, Option 3

Option 2

- As 3 receives the ball, 5 takes two steps out and sets a pick for 2.
- 2 cuts off pick from 5 and gets pass from 3 for layup.
- If 1 defender drops back to help 2, 3 quickly passes to 1 for an open three-point shot (fig. 9.31).

Option 3

- As 2 cuts off 5 pick, 3 looks to get him the ball on the cut.
- If 2 doesn't get the ball, 5 quickly cuts to hoop for pass from 3 and layup.
- 2 continues to cut and roll out on the weak side (fig. 9.32).

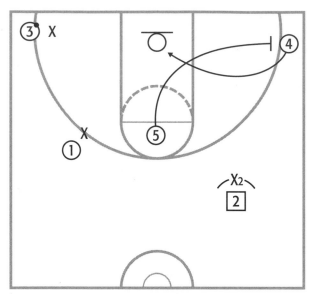

Figure 9.33   Box-and-One Offense, Option 4

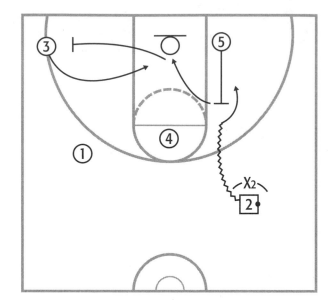

Figure 9.34   Box-and-One Offense, Option 5

Option 4

- If 3 doesn't pass to 2 or 5, 5 sets pick for 4.
- 3 passes to 4 underneath the basket for a layup (fig. 9.33).

Option 5

- 5 sets a pick for 2.
- 2 dribbles off 5 pick for layup or jump shot.
- 5 rolls to basket; if he is not open, 5 sets pick for 3.
- 2 looks for shot or pass to 5 or 3 (fig. 9.34).

Developing the Tricks of the Trade

Last-Minute Tactics with Proven Results

When you coach a particular sport for a long time, you begin to develop some consistency, based on trial and error, on what it takes to win. As a young coach, you spend the majority of your time learning what not to do, by making mistakes, as opposed to what you are supposed to do. Eventually, you settle down and get into a consistent rhythm and structure that you follow in coaching. When it starts to work and things finally start to click, you stick with it and become very systematic, like most good coaches, and stay with what works.

If I were to pinpoint what makes a successful basketball team, I would have to break it down into seven categories: preparation, teamwork, percentage shooting, pressure defense, a solid fast break, good passing, and, of course, execution.

PREPARATION

If you have read to this point, you can probably tell that I have a checklist for everything and follow it precisely. When I was coaching, every item on a list had to be covered before the season started. Before every game, my coaches and I prepared our team for anything and everything that the opposing coaches had shown so far and, more important, what they hadn't shown but might use. Ask any coach what his biggest fear is in the business, and he will say not being prepared for everything. This comes with scouting, which I will thoroughly explain later in this chapter.

TEAMWORK

Throughout my years of coaching, I became convinced that a good high school team could beat an all-star team. The all-star team will rarely display teamwork. That is why a team that displays togetherness on the court can beat a team that has more talented players but lacks cohesiveness.

PERCENTAGE SHOOTING

The importance of taking high-percentage shots is something that your players must learn. Once they get into the habit of developing patience and looking for the open shots, they will make more baskets, and, in turn, you will win more games. My teams led the league in shooting percentage for more than half of the forty years I coached.

PRESSURE DEFENSE

Pressure defense will wear your opponents down, slowly but surely. An important part of this type of defense is keeping pressure on your opponent while rotating and using your sixth and seventh reserve players as fresh legs while your starters rest. Although I have emphasized the superiority of putting together a pressure, man-to-man–oriented team, there are times when other defenses should be played. For example, with ten seconds to go and the game on the line, your opponent has the ball and calls time-out to set up a last-second shot. I have been successful in changing from a man-to-man defense to a zone while the other coach is setting up a man-to-man offensive play. At other times, in similar situations, we would set up a box-and-one defense on their star shooter. Sometimes, to really confuse them, we would set up a box-and-one on their point guard.

FAST BREAK

As I explained earlier, if the fast break is executed properly, it will give you seven to ten baskets per game. Some coaches think that if their team doesn't have the speed, they cannot run a fast break. They are wrong. The New Jersey Nets are a prime example of this. They are not the quickest team in the NBA, but they release their point guard Jason Kidd early to run down the court. At the high school level, the point guard is usually the quickest player, so release him early and get him down the court for a head start.

GOOD PASSING

To make a pass properly, your team must fake a pass properly. The one sure way of beating pressure defenses is to move the ball. Your players must understand that if their teammate is cutting behind a screen for a jump shot, the pass should not be made until that player pivots, squares to the basket, and gets ready to shoot. The pass should always be thrown chest high. A pass low and at his knees will throw his shot off. Your point guard must learn the strengths and weaknesses of his teammates. He must know who can catch his passes and what type of passes they can use to their advantage. Obviously, this is the type of chemistry that can be developed over time.

EXECUTION

Obviously, all of these components are worthless unless they are executed properly. Timing is essential, and each player must understand the offense and defense completely. Players must also master the fundamentals of the game. Without fundamentals, the Xs and Os are worthless.

SCOUTING: EXPECT THE UNEXPECTED

I have already touched on the importance of preparation as a coach and the necessity to dissect an opponent's strengths and weaknesses before you line up and play them. Too many coaches don't spend enough time on this aspect of the game. You have to be able to know what to expect and when to expect it. But, more important, you have to know what not to expect in certain situations. This is the true essence of a good coach, being able to prepare your team for what could happen, not necessarily what would happen when you face your opponent.

In reality, you never truly know what to expect, so you have to prepare for the unexpected. The best way to do this is a method called "self-scouting." This was always a surefire method of evaluating our own team. All professional organizations do this with their coaches, but today it is becoming more and more popular in high school athletics. By taking the point of view of an opponent and breaking down your game film as if you were scouting yourself, you check your own tendencies—such as your play-calling habits, the personnel that you use, your strengths, and your weaknesses. When this is completed, you can even go so far, if time permits, as to file a scouting report on your basketball team. This helps tremendously when preparing to play an opponent, because you are able to see what they are seeing on film and at least you can anticipate what they may do.

Each season, my coaches and I scouted the preseason state and county tournament favorite at least four times. We did so because this was the team the experts said was the best in the area. We wanted to find out on our own what these players were all about. For one, we liked to make our own judgment on what the buzz was all about, and we also figured that we would play the team eventually, so we wanted to get some formidable scouting in.

If our opponent had an excellent offense, from midseason until we played them in the tournament, we used and ran their offense during the last fifteen minutes of each practice. We got to know their offense as well as they did and eventually started to run it better than they did. Because of our preparation, if we met that team in tournament, we had an edge, and a bag of tricks in case we wanted to give them a taste of their own medicine by running their offense. We also ran their out-of-bounds plays and anything else they did well.

When sending your assistant coaches to scout for you, there is essential information you want them to look for. Here are ten points to look for and some questions that must be answered when scouting an upcoming opponent:

1. What type of man-to-man defense do they run?
   - Are they are a pressure or sagging defense?
   - Are they a full-court or half-court defense?
   - What players hit the gaps looking for steals?
   - Do they play in front of or behind the post players when fighting for positioning down low?
   - Do they double on the ball?
   - Do they box out?
   - Do they reach in for steals or play back?
   - Do they attempt to draw charges?
   - What players draw charges?
2. What type of zone defense do they run?
   - Do they run a number setup like a 2-1-2, 3-2, 2-3, 1-2-2, or 1-3-1?
   - Do they like to set up a box-and-one on the opponent's best player?
   - Do they run a matchup zone, where they play a man-to-man principle but rotate assignments and switch men?
   - Is the zone a packed-in zone, with no perimeter help for outside shots?
   - What slides do they employ for defense?
   - Do they box out?
   - Do they fast-break off the zone?
   - How does their defense rotate?
3. Do they release early for layups?
   - Some teams like to head down the court as soon as the shot goes up. Does this team?
   - Do they send the big men like the forwards down first ?
   - Do they "chippy-hang"? Meaning, do they run down the other end of the court as their teammates get the rebound?
4. Do they fast-break?
   - Does their point guard crash the boards for a rebound while their big men sprint down the court?
   - Does their point guard push the ball up the court as soon as he handles the rebound?
5. What type of offense do they run?
6. What are their out-of-bounds plays?
7. Chart their top seven players according to size and ability to provide for some matchups.
8. List and analyze their top scorers.
   - Are they right- or left-handed?
   - Are they inside or outside players?
   - What are their tendencies?
   - What are their abilities as scorers?
   - Who are their leaders and who are their role players?
   - Who gets the ball in pressure situations?
   - Who gets it when the game is on the line?
   - What are their weaknesses as ball players?
9. What are their press defenses?
10. What are their press offenses?

This would be the type of format or checklist we would follow when we put together our scouting report. As a result, our game breakdowns would give us a lot of success because all our previous questions coming into the game we were scouting had been answered. I remember one tournament game in particular where the number-one-seeded team had an exceptional thirty-point-per-game scorer. While scouting,

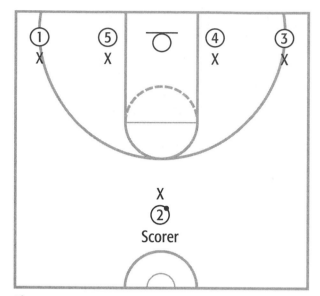

Figure 10.1

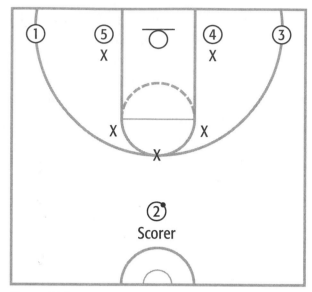

Figure 10.2

we noticed that teams would play a box-and-one on him, with the same defensive player guarding him. This might have been a decent solution for the first couple minutes of the game, but as the game wore on he would identify the defenders' weaknesses and begin to exploit them. Also, the defender would get tired during the game, and, if he wasn't as fit as the scorer, he would most likely surrender some points when the game was on the line.

With this in mind, we decided that we would pick up the player at full court and press him even when he didn't have the ball. Each quarter, we would switch the defender, just so he got a different look and couldn't settle in. Eventually, with fresh legs on our side, we wore him down. The opposing team ran their four pattern plays during the first, second, and third quarters, and in the fourth quarter they went into their game-winning offense by putting their thirty-point scorer at the point and ran a 1-4 low offense, isolating him at the top of the key (fig. 10.1).

When they switched into their 1-4 low offense, we switched into our 3-2 tight zone (fig. 10.2). As a result the scorer was frustrated and took some forced shots. In the end, we beat the number-one seed.

CHAPTER

11

The Other Season

Turning Your Program into a Twelve-Month-a-Year Effort That Will Produce Enormous Results Off-Season

To have a successful basketball program, it is essential to view your off-season as your "other season." From the day the season ends, in late February, until it begins again, the day after Thanksgiving, you must look at this as your second season. Successful coaches and players must have the mentality that there is never a time when they are completely away from the game of basketball. This is not to say that coaches should commit their players to an extremely vigorous agenda where they spend two to three hours a day on the hardwood, but they cannot let them get out of shape, either.

As a basketball coach, I didn't get involved in any other sports because I wanted to make sure I was spending the time necessary to develop our program. Obviously, you can't always expect that type of commitment from athletes with interests other than the game of basketball, so the time you spend with them has to be valuable. I have always stressed the importance of playing other sports during the fall and spring, under one condition: The player should be committed to playing that particular sport; it shouldn't be something that is done to "pass the time" during the off-season, when there is no basketball. If a player is going to put his time into something, it had better be worth it. This is an extremely valuable lesson coaches can teach players. Many athletes fall into the routine of running track or cross-country just to keep themselves busy, instead of working hard at the sport.

My yearly off-season program was divided into four parts:

1. Player and body development
2. Open-house workouts
3. Summer leagues
4. Summer camps

PLAYER DEVELOPMENT

If our players chose to go out for other sports—especially cross-country, spring track, and soccer—we encouraged it. Being a former cross-country runner myself, I know firsthand that it builds endurance and tremendous conditioning that can be used on the basketball court. Spring track helps to develop speed and keeps players in shape. A lot of the fast-twitch muscle development that can be honed in events such as spring track can be useful in a game like basketball, where players are constantly stopping and starting and changing direction. Soccer not only builds endurance and gets players in shape but also toughens them and, because of the open-field contact, gives them a more aggressive style in hoops.

For players not involved in another sport, the preseason starts after the last state tournament game in March. We started this early for body development purposes. We would set up a weight-lifting and workout regimen for these players after school for about two hours a day, three days a week. I would have one of my assistants supervise the weight room to make sure the players were working out. Basketball, unlike a sport like football, doesn't require much heavy, short, explosive lifting, so we would work a lot on exercises designed to develop reflexes and long-term movements. The last thing you want to do is hinder your players' athleticism and movement by putting strain on their muscles. Lower weight, with numerous repetitions, in our exercises is what we were looking for. Below, I give an example of our traditional workout day.

OPEN-HOUSE WORKOUTS

Working in both a private and public school, I would usually hold an open house for potential students entering high school to get a firsthand look at our school and my basketball program. It is a great experience and a good tool for becoming acquainted with the younger players who will be coming up through the ranks. We did this successfully for a number of years. And to prevent eager questioning by parents, students, and alumni about when we would start our open-house workouts, we decided to start the day after daylight savings time began, in April.

We held these open houses on Monday, Wednesday, and Friday, from 6:00 to 8:00 P.M. We even allowed parents who had some basketball ability to work out with us and run through our drills. It was fun and became something of a father-son event. Dads were getting in condition with their sons. We also encouraged graduate players to return and work out with us as well. They were home from school by now, which enabled them to keep in shape for their college teams and also gave us a chance to compete against excellent athletes. We would continue this program until the start of basketball practice.

During the early part of spring, we played indoors, using our gym. We divided our group into four sections: freshmen and sophomores, juniors and seniors, and parents. As soon as weather allowed, we moved outside and worked out in the fresh air of our outdoor basketball courts on the playground. The following are the rules we instituted for these workouts:

6:00–6:05: Team draft or selection of teams for half-court five-on-five games, up to seven points. The tallest players act as captains and make selections per court. Each team must have one male parent, and parents will play against parents, never a parent against a student.

6:05–7:15: The round-robin games will be half-court only. Winners play winners; losers play losers. Additional players not on a team or arriving late can play by virtue of a foul-shooting contest, with the loser sitting.

7:15–8:00: This is were we come together as a unit. We work on two full-court areas, with the parents sitting and watching. On court one, alumni players and our best players battle. On court two, underclassmen play full court.

Coach's Note: Some states do not allow the coach to attend the open houses. In this case, I would allow my captain to run the workouts, but only if parents were present in the gym.

SUMMER CAMPS

For a couple of reasons, this is, by far, the most vital and instrumental part of your off-season workout regimen. For one, you are able to showcase your athletes against other squads in the area. Second, if you do this correctly, it can be a major marketing tool, as well as an excellent fundraiser, to get your program on the map and keep it going strong. The more exposure you get with these camps, the better your team is represented. You want to make sure you run a first-class camp, because you are placing your school's reputation on the line. If the camp reflects positively on your program, you will continue to get the support of parents and administrators you need to win basketball games.

At each school where I coached, we decided to start our own one-week day camp on a local level. Usually half of our campers would be from our program. The ages of campers ranged from nine to eighteen for boys and twelve to eighteen for girls. We accomplished a number of things through these camps, but I learned that the most important were

- Improving the fundamental play of our students
- Increasing the motivation aspect of basketball in our school and in our local community
- Giving coaches a greater insight into our players' strengths, weaknesses, and attitudes
- Introducing our coaches, school, and facilities to our elementary grade students
- Providing a local camp for basketball players ages eight to eighteen and giving them something productive to do during the summer

Before you decide to run a camp for your program, you must decide what type of camp you want to start. For example, choices include:

- A camp catering exclusively to your students
- A camp open to the public

We decided to start an "open-to-the-public" camp. It gives us better competition, greater flexibility, and more campers, enabling us to create three divisions: college division (ages eight to twelve), ABA division (ages thirteen and fourteen), and NBA division (ages fifteen to eighteen).

We initially had a low-budget camp without frills, and, through word of mouth and advertising, we progressed to a superior status. To be competitive with other camps in your area, you must build additional activities or incentives into your camp as enrollment increases. The ideal number of campers in a first year is sixty-five. This will allow you to set up three divisions with four teams in each division.

Budget Services

Forming a summer camp can be quite costly, especially when you don't know exactly what you're doing, which was the case when I first started running my own. To get your camp off the ground, you have to be a mover and shaker at the beginning. Here are a few tips experience taught us along the way:

- Ask your local sporting-goods stores whether they would like to become cosponsors of the camp. They can donate camp T-shirts with their logo on the back and your logo on the front.
- Ask your local trophy shop to donate plaques, trophies, or prizes to your cause.
- Contact athletic footwear companies such as Adidas, Nike, and Converse to notify them. They will normally supply you with free guest speakers, free posters, and T-shirts that can be used as prizes.
- Contact and send a press release to the local newspaper. If you have developed a strong positive relationship with the sportswriters, they will be glad to insert camp information in their columns. Nurturing relationships with sportswriters is just as important in numerous other circumstances, too.
- Contact local businesses in your area to help defray the cost of brochures. Insurance companies, for example, will pay part of the cost if their logo or message is on the brochure.

Advertising

When putting together a brochure to advertise your summer camp, keep in mind that you want to make it as noticeable as possible, but still clear and concise. Take your time and use a little marketing sense when it comes to this because the brochure has to be an attention-grabber. You want to sell yourself as a coach and your program as a success. Make sure to feature whatever credentials your school has to offer (state championships, league championships, one or two excellent players, or even great facilities) on the front fold of the brochure. This is what people will see right away when they get it in the mail.

You should also have a couple of pictures of yourself, your players, and your facilities so potential campers can see what they can expect of you and your camp. It is very important, especially for kids, to be able to visualize you. When they arrive for camp the first day, they will have some sense of familiarity with you. More important, you have to send a message to parents in the brochure. They are entrusting you with their children, and it is an investment for them to do so; they deserve to hear what type of reward they will get in return. You have to assure them of insurance and liability coverage in case a camper is injured, and you have to provide them with contact numbers in case something goes wrong. This will help you establish a level of trust or assurance with the parents. In return, you will receive their support and admiration. In most cases, they are the ones who have more of an impact on you keeping or losing your job—more so than even the administration. This is an example of a letter I sent out to parents in my brochures for summer camp:

Dear Parents:

With the excellent facilities of the _____ school at our disposal, we intend to teach the fundamentals of basketball. We feature outstanding coaches and teachers from throughout New Jersey.

There also will be a heavy emphasis on the motivation, attitude, discipline, and conditioning of our young athletes. I can assure you that my staff and I will work just as hard to develop your son or daughter as we do with all the young men and women in our program.

Thank you in advance,

Coach Bill Kuchar

Some other messages to include in your brochure or advertisement are as follows:

- On the cover, note your cosponsors prominently. Also, have an action photo to catch the reader's attention.
- In the application, include a section for the parents to sign concerning medical emergencies.
- Discuss the purpose of the camp and activities.
- Include information about the camp director, coaches, prestigious camp alumni, and so forth.
- Point out features of the camp and list whatever equipment is required.
- Create a letter acknowledging receipt of application and check. This is very important because people want to know where their money is going. To help parents set up car pools, we always included a note on the bottom left of this letter with the names and phone numbers of other accepted campers from the applicants' area.
- Have a space for any notes as well as a copy of camp rules.
- Include an evaluation sheet that will be used for all campers. Each coach is required to fill in and present this "report card" to his players on the last day of camp. It should give some type of assessment of a camper's strengths and weaknesses. In my coaching experience, the report card was always a fan favorite.

Activities and Schedules

What type of activities you plan depends solely on the availability of the facilities you have. We had the fortune of utilizing four outdoor courts for five-on-five, three-on-three, and one-on-one competition. While six teams are competing outdoors, six teams are at what we called "stations" inside the gym. It takes a tremendous amount of preparation to make sure everything is going on track and that there is no confusion. Because you want them to get the most out of their experience, make sure that campers are involved in some type of activity throughout the day. Because we couldn't physically have 150 campers shooting hoops at the same time, we developed these stations and drills as a supplemental workout:

- Shooting instruction
- Dribbling instruction with training classes
- Boxing-out
- Passing drills
- Rebounding and outlet passing
- Defense
- "H-O-R-S-E" and "Beat the Pro" for prizes
- Instructional films by our sponsors
- One-on-one coaching
- Various highlight-reel entertainment—college, NBA, etc.

Awards

Young people are competitive by nature, but they still need some type of encouragement or reward in these games. Although you don't want to single out one particular camper, we tried to reward as many participators as possible, regardless of ability or skill level. To do this, we always had an awards ceremony on the last day of camp and would invite all the parents to attend. We would usually present rewards for the following types of achievements:

- Championship plaques to five-on-five winners
- Ten trophies to the college division (eight- to twelve-year-olds)
- Ten trophies to the ABA division (thirteen- and fourteen-year-olds)
- Ten trophies to the NBA division (fifteen- to eighteen-year-olds)
- Nine trophies to the three-on-three winners—three divisions
- Five trophies to one-on-one champs—five divisions
- Twelve trophies, four per division, for most valuable camper, most improved camper, hustle award, and sportsmanship award
- Five trophies for foul-shooting championships and "Beat the Pro" winners

Summary

Most camps are geared toward profit. We did not subscribe to this approach, but we were still able to sell out every year because we produced a fun and comfortable learning atmosphere for players. In turn, players were drawn to our camp every year because of quality coaching, quality guest speakers, a free basketball as a giveaway, trophies, prizes, free insurance, and free T-shirts.

We kept the campers busy with what they came to us for, instruction in how to play fundamentally sound basketball, and we rewarded them for outstanding performance and positive attitudes. From the standpoint of motivation and skills learned, this camp greatly benefited and enhanced our basketball program and only helped us develop our program into the best that it could be.

CHAPTER

12

Building a Dynasty

Making the Constant Commitment to Turning an Average Team into a Championship Dynasty

Any time a new coach takes over the reins of a program—especially one that has been proven to be underachieving or less than promising—the first thing he or she must do is build a foundation. Like any other enterprise, it is essential to start from the bottom and work up. As simplistic as it may sound, many first-year head coaches have delusions of grandeur, expecting to turn a perennial cellar-dweller into a powerhouse right away. Like the cliché "Rome wasn't built in a day," great basketball programs are not built overnight.

When I got my first head coaching job, I thought I could work miracles almost instantly. The school's basketball team had just finished struggling through its first year, winning only two games. As a gung-ho twenty-four-year-old coming right out of my collegiate career, I believed we could win the league title and compete for a state championship from the outset. What I didn't realize, or neglected to take into consideration, was who I had playing for me, who I had coaching with me, who was looking out for me in the building, and, perhaps, who wanted me to fail. Unfortunately, in the realm of high school athletics, politics in the program are as important as the games you play. I learned at an early age whom to trust, whom to talk to, and whom I needed in my corner to revive a sleeping giant—and do it the right way.

Of course, hindsight is always 20-20, and as I look back at my coaching career, it seems obvious that there were important elements that contributed to my success, most of which I've learned through trial and error.

EDUCATE YOURSELF

Too many young coaches come into the coaching ranks thinking they know everything there is to know about the sport they coach. Certainly what this profession does not need are more hotheaded, ego-driven, totalitarian coaches who think they are going to reinvent the wheel—or the basketball. There are more than enough of these sorts of coaches to go around. Even the most successful, proven coaches admit that they are constantly learning and evolving as coaches. We are all students of the game. Every day we must strive to learn something new. It will not only benefit our well-being, but also the progress of the players we coach.

As a coach, I felt it was necessary to attend as many basketball clinics or lectures as possible. There are plenty of outstanding coaches to learn from in every area of this country, and the minute you as a coach lose the desire to learn, you have lost the desire to coach. Purchase basketball books and videos, especially on the aspects of the game where you feel you are weak or need to improve. My basketball library at my home takes up a whole bedroom in my basement, and it continues to grow even after my retirement from the game.

All good coaches need to be like sponges, absorbing as much information as possible in order to better themselves. Another way to improve your knowledge of the game is to get out and observe critical games in your area. Try to follow influential coaches and their teams throughout your area, and scout them when you can. Chances are, you'll learn something you didn't know before, and you'll make some valuable contacts down the road that you may need in accomplishing what should be your most important goal—getting your kids to college.

HIRING YOUR HORSES

If it is true that a jockey is only as good as the horse he rides, then head coaches are only as good as the people they have working with them. Notice how I use the phrase "working with them," not "working for them." Although it is important that as a head coach you oversee all of the aspects of your program, to be a successful team you must be able to work together with your assistants. These are the people you will hold most accountable for the success of your program when things are going well.

As a head coach, it is important to not be a dictator, micromanaging every detail of your program. Your assistants should be a reflection of you, a point I will elaborate on later. Delegate duties to each and every one of them so everything runs as smoothly and efficiently as possible. No one on earth has the time or resources to handle every part of the program, from ordering equipment to calling parents and reserving gymnasium time. Take some of the best head coaches in the college basketball game, such as Mike Krzyzewski at Duke and Jim Calhoun at UConn. They all have quality assistants who have been with them for years. In each case, the head coach has developed a trust or partnership with his assistant. Their loyalty will be beyond question, which is the greatest asset a coach can have. Aside from all the technical operations of getting ready to play a basketball game, there are areas such as discipline, academics, and publicity that should be monitored by your assistants. You don't want to give them too much authority, where questions of your credibility could arise, but you don't want to treat them like soldiers, either. If you do this, you will lose them faster than you can hire them.

Throughout my coaching tenure, I was fortunate to work with quality assistants who were also quality people. One of the things I learned, especially at the high school level, is that it is more important to hire exceptional people with good character than those with exceptional knowledge of the game. You can always teach them Xs and Os, but you can't teach them how to respond to players and, more important, how to get them to want to play for you. Having said this, it is important to hire some coaches with prior playing experience, either at the collegiate or high school level, or with previous coaching experience. Usually, if you are an offensive-minded coach, as I was, you want to hire a coach with a considerable background in defense. Or if you stress defense as a coach, it would make sense to offset your personality by selecting someone who is used to running diverse offensive sets. Just like in football, where there are two separate coaches who run the defense and the offense, it would help if you had someone with proven knowledge in both of those aspects of the game.

As the success of your program and your reputation builds, the reputation of your assistants does as well, which at times is unfortunate for a head coach. Naturally, assistants get hungry and want head coaching jobs of their own, making them targets for other schools to steal. I had five longtime assistant coaches who worked for me during my forty years, most of whom went on to become head coaches of their own teams. Joe Pope coached for me for ten years, eventually leaving to take the head job at Hudson Catholic in Jersey City. Pete Romano was my assistant for ten years and then took over at Saint Mary's when I left to take the head job at St. Joe's. Rich Lee worked with me for twelve years before leaving to be an assistant at the college level at Stevens Tech in Hoboken. John Hoops (no pun intended) worked with me in the scouting department for twenty years and then retired from the game. Howard McCallum was my assistant for eleven years, when he decided to retire and move out of the area. So as you start to develop a reputation for your basketball program, your players and you will not be the only ones to get noticed.

DEVELOPING TRUST WITH YOUR ADMINISTRATION

Next to your coaching staff and your players, the school administration should be the most essential part of building a program. The way you should look at this situation is that they took the time and consideration to trust you by hiring you as a head coach, so they should command your respect. They are entrusting you to represent their school with the utmost dignity and respect, and you should treat them in the same manner. Some new coaches get caught up playing politics with administrators and wind up cutting them out of the loop of what's going on with the team. For the most part, excellent administrators want to see their school succeed; it looks good for the school, and it gives the institution a positive reputation around the area. In the simplest terms, a positive reputation for you as coach and your program leads to the influx of talented players, which leads to more wins, which eventually turns one or two twenty-win seasons into fifteen to twenty twenty-win seasons.

I've worked in parochial and private schools for my entire coaching career. In the private school sector, financial aid is extremely important. For a coach, the one benefit private schools have over public institutions is the option of selecting his own players, provided they are compatible with the atmosphere or academic standing of the school, which is why your working relationship with your headmaster/principal should be solid. There are many talented but poor players who want to play basketball. If your principal is willing to give some financial aid to a potential athlete with good grades, consider yourself lucky, and don't do anything to rock the boat with your higher-ups.

The truth is, you can be as important to the school administration as they are to you. What you do as a coach on the court can directly affect their jobs as administrators. Success breeds success. It works both ways. For example, after winning my first state championship at Saint Mary's High School in 1967, I was amazed at the phone calls I began to receive from parents wanting to send their sons to the school just to play basketball for me. Not only did I have an increasing demand from new prospects the following year wanting to come to the school, but the enrollment of the student body rose by 30 percent. After our second state championship, two years later, our school (for the first time) had a waiting list for admissions, and it was a direct result of what we did on the basketball court.

KEEPING WINNING FUN

Finally, it's important to realize that winning is contagious. As euphoric as the feeling gets when you are winning, it can just as quickly consume you, sapping every positive feeling you have. Winning is like a drug. Once you get a taste of it, you crave more, and usually you will stop at nothing to get it. It's the rite of passage for every true competitor—the thirst that is never satisfied. But you have to know exactly how to control that thirst. Too many coaches compromise their ethics, morals, and character just to keep winning, to stay on top. Unfortunately, in coaching you're only as good as your last game, and as baseball great Satchel Paige put it, "Don't look back. Something might be gaining on you."

When I started coaching, my personal goal, much like everyone else's at this level, was to win a state championship. I did everything in my power to reach that goal. When I finally accomplished it, my goal became winning two state championships, then three, then four. That's how it starts. Winning is a habit, and if you ask any coach at any level, he or she will tell you that it takes a lot more to stay on top than to get there. It's always tougher being the hunted than the hunter.

One of the things we did to keep the edge was to run summer camps for potential players. I ran summer camps at every school I coached, and it became a great resource for scouting potential players as well as fine-tuning the skills of the players I already had. In my career, many of my most outstanding players I met at these camps. The youngest kids we had were around nine and ten years old. By the time they turned fourteen and were ready to enter high school, I had already developed a trusting, paralleled relationship with them. If you are successful running camps, players will have learned a tremendous amount from you and your staff and will want to play for you. At one point at St. Joe's High School, in Metuchen, we had an enrollment of more than 160 campers, many of them wanting to play for us.

Summer leagues are another good way to elevate your program. Although it is not mandatory, and high school students usually have other obligations, your players must be told how important it is that they attend these games. I would always look for the most competitive league to enroll my students in. It would serve as a true test for our program as well as an evaluation period for myself to see who did their homework that summer and who wanted to get on the court the following winter. Usually, I would have enough kids to enter two full teams as well as give my upcoming junior varsity players some real-game experience.

As for potential players, I have always hosted a grammar school basketball tournament. What better way to observe and acquaint yourself and your staff with the best players in your area? Start out with an eight-team tournament and build to a sixteen-team setup. Charge a reasonable entrance fee to cover officials and trophies. Have your staff or players work the concession stand, selling your T-shirts for extra money and additional revenue for the school and program.

Bring in quality officials and give out quality trophies. Make sure it's run professionally, a top-class operation. Make your tournament the best in the area, so kids want to come. This is a perfect time to do some quality networking. Send season passes for the grammar school coaches to attend your regular-season games. Be on a first-name basis with those coaches—you'll turn them into fans of your program quicker than you would think. Also invite youth group and boys' club coaches to attend your practice sessions and give them some of the freshmen offense and fundamentals that you use. It's your reputation that's on the line. If people see that you run your camp in a dignified and productive manner, they can only assume the same about the way you run your program.

Over the course of my coaching tenure, I was fortunate enough to have placed 130 players into college programs. Attain the reputation of not only being a good coach, but also a quality person who looks out and cares for his players. I spent every off-season of my career writing letters and sending films to colleges and universities all over the country to make sure my players had the opportunity of getting a higher education. When you combine a good coaching reputation with your ability to help your players go to the next level, the players will continuously come and you will have an ongoing cycle of players going to the next level and starting their college careers.

CHAPTER 13

Developing Teamwork

Eliminating Distractions for the Greater Good of the Team

Most people know that coaching is a form of teaching. What you're teaching is irrelevant. Whether it's basketball, biology, or basket weaving, the goal is to convey a lesson to your pupils. That is what sums teaching up in a nutshell—giving lifelong lessons and relating them to the material being taught. Over the years, I came to the conclusion that the importance of instruction does not lie so much in what I'm teaching as how I am teaching it. Obviously, some are better than others in their teaching methods, but all strive to get their point across in the best way possible.

One of my role models in the coaching profession has been Bill Parcells, who is now the head football coach of the Dallas Cowboys. In my mind, he, along with John Wooden, is the master teacher—a dying breed in the world of sports. When I say "master teachers," I mean individuals who have an innate ability to teach, to hold court over a group of young people who hang on the teacher's every word. Master teachers develop an immeasurable amount of trust and honesty with the people they coach. As far as I'm concerned, a person like Bill Parcells can coach anything, and the world of football is lucky to have him. I enjoy reading about other teacher-coaches who follow in this mold, people like Dick Vermeil of the Kansas City Chiefs and, of course, Mike Krzyzewski at Duke. What I enjoy most is hearing former players talk about their coaches long after their tenure has ended. As a coach it is then, long after your time has passed with them, that you see the impression you made on players.

One of the things that makes Bill Parcells a great coach is that he treats each player differently. By this I'm not inferring that he is unfair, but that he knows how to deal with certain types of players. Who else can tame a personality like Keyshawn Johnson? The toughest thing in coaching is assembling different types of players, with various backgrounds and personalities, and making them play together with unity and cohesiveness. Parcells is the master of this, and nearly every player he has coached has stayed with him for his entire career. Parcells has the innate ability to get his players to want to work hard for him because he gets his point across in some way, shape, or form to all of his players.

I firmly believe in being fair, but I also believe in treating each player differently. For example, if a player had a habit of showing up late for team meetings and had a pattern of what coaches call "exaggerating the truth" and missed practice for an unbelievable reason, my punishment would probably be more severe than it would be for a disciplined and hardworking player who had never missed a day of practice or a meeting the entire time I coached him. I think the key to coaching is knowing how to respond to these different types of personalities. While you can't be lenient all the time, by the same token, you can't have tunnel vision. You have to realize that these players are high school students, not professional athletes, and you need to remember that there are priorities in their lives other than the game of basketball. To be a successful teacher, you have to take this into consideration. Chances are, you will be a father figure to these students, and you may be giving them guidance they don't get at home.

For the first half of my coaching tenure, I worked in an inner city. There were many other aspects of my players' personal lives that I had to get accustomed to before I could begin teaching them about shooting a jump shot or setting a pick. Because I was a city kid myself who went through the same circumstances, I was able to relate to some of their issues. This is one of the main reasons got I my first head-coaching job when I was only twenty-four. The school administration that hired me realized that it is more important to make a difference on students' lives than to teach them about basketball, because many of them didn't have any structure at home and had to get it someplace. Basketball was their release, and if they learned something that would influence their lives in a positive way, it might help them in bigger ways than basketball.

Early in my career, I decided that I wanted to base the success of my program on three main components—discipline, attitude, and motivation. I felt that if I had all these tangibles, winning would work itself out.

DISCIPLINE

Like many other coaches, the first thing I had to do when I got the job was to give some type of structure in our program, and this starts with discipline. Although most of my players knew how to handle themselves, I had to make it clear that I wasn't going to tolerate any resistance, no matter who gave it. So, during my first practice, I purposely instigated an altercation with one of my star players. I criticized him for something simple, like not hustling, because I wanted to see how he'd respond. What I was doing was baiting him into having a confrontation with me, because I wanted to show the other players that, no matter who you are, nobody is bigger than the program. When he gave me the slightest bit of backtalk, I sent him to the showers early, and he went home for the day.

When the players see something like this, chances are the others will fall in line. If there is still a problem with another player, take him into your office and explain what you expect from him. If he intends to keep playing for you, warn him to change his attitude. If he continues to persist in seeing how far he can push you, suspend him for one practice and, when he returns, tell him the next suspension is final. In forty years of coaching, I never had to throw a player off the team—because I insisted on team discipline and was very firm with my players.

ATTITUDE

Once you develop a sense of team discipline, you must develop your team's attitude. I define attitude as a person's outlook or how he perceives different situations. It is vital that your team be positive, no matter what the circumstances. This is something that can be learned, and it is your job as a coach to teach it to your players. Whatever else is going on in their lives that could cause them to be negative, when they step onto that court they have to believe that they are a team of destiny, that only good things are going to happen to them. This is because eventually their attitude, not their ability, will be what propels them to greater heights in life. You determine a lot about an individual when you see how they handle adversity and obstacles. Do they sink into despair when things are going wrong, or do they face the situation and try to make the best of what they have?

I remember speaking to George Blaney, who at the time was the head coach of Holy Cross College. When he was recruiting one of my players, I started to tell him about the shooting and jumping talents of one of my players who had an interest in furthering his education at Holy Cross. Before I could finish my sales pitch about this player's abilities, Blaney said, "Before you tell me how great a player he is, tell me first about his attitude." I reiterate Coach Blaney's comments to my players at the start of every season, so there is an understanding that, no matter how good they think they are, if they don't have the right attitude, they'll never reach their true potential.

MOTIVATION

"Motivation," I believe, is the single most important word in coaching. The reason for this is a very motivated team can beat a team with more talent any day of the week. We see this all the time. First, you must impress upon your players that they must, under all circumstances, stay motivated and play together as a team.

One thing I did to motivate my teams was to leave the locker room five minutes early and turn the team over to the captain and cocaptain to address their teammates. I knew as a former player that teammates always respond better to their peers, so I used it to my advantage. When choosing a captain or cocaptain, I looked for players who were motivated and could motivate the other players. If the best-motivated player on the team is one of the players other than a captain, I called him "defensive captain" and told him it was his responsibility to get us up for the game. One of the things you have to do in a position of authority is learn how to delegate responsibilities. Players enjoy the opportunity to feel like they are a part of something. They don't want to be just soldiers.

Some coaches I have known use negative motivation. They tell their teams, "We are a better team, and we should win. If we don't win, you didn't play well." They never show accountability for themselves as coaches getting their players ready to play. Through the years, I've learned to never underestimate an opponent. If you think you are playing a weaker team, it is a greater opportunity to get the team ready to play, to avoid the ever-present chance of a letdown. Challenge your team to score twenty points in the first quarter, to get off to a fast start, and to produce steals on defense. I have seen far too many superior teams lose because of a lack of motivation.

MY MOST UNFORGETTABLE PLAYER

I want to illustrate the points about handling different players that I stressed early in this chapter by sharing a story about a player who, because of his various eccen-

tricities and antics, was a project for me as a coach. I had to treat him differently from any other player because of his demeanor, and it was a challenge to get him simply to play basketball and be a role player on our team. Without question, in my forty years, he was my most memorable player, and a valuable lesson can be learned for any coach who has to work with a student with all the ability in the world but who needs a major attitude adjustment to be a successful component of a program.

"Bobby, the Pill," was a 6'3" player who could jump four feet off the ground, run like a world-class sprinter, and shoot the threads out of the basket. He had legitimate dreams of playing in the NBA, and it was a dream that might have come to fruition had he not let his outside circumstances get in the way of his goals and his basketball ability.

In the two years he played varsity for us, we were state champions and were ranked among the top three teams in New Jersey. We played in the prestigious Monsignor King Holiday Tournament in New York, and lost to the number-one-ranked team in the country by a single point. Bobby was our star, and he knew it. His ability was second to none at the high school level, but, unfortunately, so were his antics. He had enough material to have supplied a TV sitcom.

Bobby loved to fantasize. One day he would pretend to be Kareem Abdul-Jabbar and insist on jumping center, and the next day he would be Clyde Frazer and want to play point guard. His colorful personality and the many "happenings" he perpetrated caused his teammates, our coaching staff, and the school principal to love him and hate him simultaneously, praying for the season to be over so life could be normal again.

The first time we realized Bobby was different was during a scrimmage game in Paterson, New Jersey, about twenty miles from our school. When we gathered our players together for the pregame talk, I realized Bobby was missing. When he finally sauntered onto the court, I asked him where he had been. He simply answered, "I went off by myself to meditate," and then quickly added, "Today I can really sky. I want to jump center." Now, as a side note, you have to be careful when you address someone like Bobby. He was a ticking time bomb; the slightest derogatory comment might set him off. I casually informed him that our center would jump center for the tip as planned. "Then I'll walk home after the game," he said as he turned away.

Not giving much validity to his statement—after all, we were twenty miles from home—we went on with the scrimmage. Surprisingly enough, after the game was over, we noted that Bobby was missing. We knew that we had to find him, so my two assistant coaches prowled the mean streets of Paterson by car in search of Bobby. It was almost midnight when my assistants spotted Bobby strolling leisurely down one of Paterson's most dangerous streets. My coaches pulled the car to the curb and, after a brief discussion, Bobby got into the car. The next day at practice Bobby was told that he was now required to run twenty laps before and after practice for the next two weeks.

Unfortunately, this was only the first episode. Making him run as a form of punishment didn't alleviate the problem, so I had to find other means. By midseason we were 10-0 and doing great. We were flying high, and most of our success was due to Bobby. One day I received a phone call from the school principal. She asked to see me as soon as possible. When I arrived at her office, to my surprise, I saw Bobby sitting in a chair. The principal announced that Bobby had expressed a desire to visit his mother—in Georgia! I couldn't believe my ears. In the middle of an undefeated season, our star player was going to bolt to another state for a week. When I expressed my displeasure, Bobby answered, "I haven't seen my mother in five years, and I want to go now."

Trying to appeal to his spirit, I figured the only way I could stop him was to deny any playing time when he got back, which is usually a surefire way to deter a player from doing anything that is unwanted by a coach. But still he insisted. I had enough, I was grasping at straws. I had to deliver an ultimatum. I finally said, "Okay, but you can buy yourself a one-way ticket. You won't be welcome here again." I was certain that he would change his mind. But I was only partly right. When I got home that night, I found a note waiting for me on my doorstep that read, "Dear Coach, I decided to take your advice and cancel my trip to Georgia. However, I decided to visit my brother in Atlantic City and will miss practice this weekend."

On another occasion, the news was that Walt Frazer of the New York Knickerbockers had a finger poked in his eyes and had to wear goggles for the next couple of games. The day after we heard this, and about one hour before a very important conference game, Bobby came up to me and said as seriously as he could, "Coach, I have a problem with my eyes and can't play unless you get me goggles."

Holding our heads in our hands in dismay, we tried to figure a way to appease this temperamental player so he could play to his full capacity. We needed him to play. My quick-thinking assistant coach Pete Romano ran to a nearby building, which was under construction, and somehow managed to return with a pair of badly scratched welder's goggles! Bobby was delighted. To our disbelief, the refs let him play in the game with them on and he went on to lead us to victory, scoring a season-high thirty-six points. During our next game, Bobby missed his first five shots, so he ripped off the goggles and threw them under the bench. This ended the "goggle episode."

Sometimes I wish I could forget the two most important games of my career, because Bobby may have cost us a county championship as well as a state championship. We were tied for the county championship, and a win in this particular game would have given us a berth in the title game. Our team's high scorers at the time were a 6' 6" center named Percy Anderson (a 1,000-point scorer) and Bobby. The opposing coach decided to play a triangle and two, but the twist was that he decided not to have anyone cover Bobby.

The coach put up a triangle in the three-second area to contain Anderson and left Bobby completely uncovered. I take my hat off to this coach, because his tactic was truly inspired. Bobby felt slighted by the coach's neglect of him and refused to shoot the ball—from sixteen feet away. When I called time-out and brought Bobby over to question this disturbing scenario, his response was, "Hey, man! I can't shoot if no one is playing me." Because of Bobby's no-shot-if-not-guarded philosophy, we lost a close game and a chance for the county title.

Finally, the following year in 1976, we were playing legendary coach Bob Hurley's St. Anthony's team from Jersey City in the state championship game. This was Bobby's senior year, and the score was tied with ten seconds left in the game. Our opponent was attempting to freeze the ball and take the last shot. St. Anthony's called time-out to set up a game-winning final shot. During the time-out, I explained to our team that if they got the last shot, because of their abundance of talent, St. Anthony's had a very good chance of winning the game. So, I wanted the defender on the second pass to go for the steal.

The ball was passed inbounds by a St. Anthony's player, and on the second pass Bobby stole the ball and drove the length of the court. With two seconds to go, Bobby dunked the ball! The crowd went wild. Unfortunately, what the crowd did not know was that dunking was prohibited by New Jersey high school basketball rules, so the referees called a technical foul on Bobby and with one second remaining, St. Anthony's made a free throw and won the state championship. After the game, with his teammates and about 3,000 spectators ready to end his life, Bobby was again among the missing. Bobby did not attend school for the next three days.

When I finally met with Bobby a week later and asked him why he decided to dunk the ball rather than finger roll it into the basket, with eyes twinkling, as he remembered that magical moment, he responded, "Coach, with the crowd screaming like that I was up there soaring with the eagles, and I had to jam it down."

Safe to say I didn't see "the Pill" much after graduation, but about two years later I received a phone call from him. He was in his sophomore year at Ramapo College in New Jersey, and they had just lost their basketball coach. He had spoken to the athletic director, recommending me for the job, and wanted me to come in for an interview. Shaking my head once again in disbelief, I quietly said, "No, thanks," and hung up the phone. Bobby went on to graduate from college and hold down an excellent job. Last time I spoke with him, he had two sons. I'll never forget the impact he had on me as a coach, and, although it eventually gave me plenty of gray hairs, because of him I learned quickly how to handle certain types of players and get them to play for the greater good of the team.

HANDLING NONPLAYER-RELATED DISTRACTIONS

As the head coach of a program, regardless of the sport, you are expected to handle problems within your team. I have already touched on types of player-related issues that must be dealt with internally. Now I will turn to outside obstacles that can have a negative effect on the disposition of your team. I was lucky enough to spend forty years coaching a sport that I love. Getting up to go to work was never hard for me. Unfortunately, I let some minor distractions get in the way of my enjoyment, and for the most part it dealt directly with parental involvement and their insistence on running my program the way they felt it should be run.

The reason why I chose to include this as a segment in my book is because it is a serious issue in the world of high school athletics, and all coaches must learn how to deal with the persistence of some parents. It starts in Little League, with the ageless scenario of the parent criticizing the coach because his child doesn't play, and it continues all the way through the high school ranks until they get to college, when children are forcefully separated from their parents. I've learned through the years that this problem never really subsides unless you fix it right away, and you set the precedent that it is *your* team and you will run it *your* way.

In my forty years of coaching, the demographics of my students have changed. I coached at an inner-city district for seventeen years where most of my players came from broken homes or single-parent situations and were forced to grow up at an early age. I coached twelve years in a middle-income district where most of my students' parents were hardworking blue-collar individuals who struggled to make ends meet. I also coached for ten years in an upper-middle-class environment where my players were fortunate enough to come from relative wealth and were able to pay large amounts of money to attend private schools. Although the types of students have changed throughout the years, there has been one constant—the involvement of pushy parents.

Some parents will start out by telling you how much they know about the game and what great players they were in high school. They will then get into what they think you are doing wrong with your program. They will say things like, "My kid is not getting enough playing time," or, "Why is that player starting before my kid?" Each complaint has to be handled tactfully and firmly, emphasizing that you are the coach, and they pay you to make the decisions. For one thing, I would strongly suggest that you try not to talk to a disgruntled parent after a tough loss—nothing good ever comes out of these situations. You're upset, and they are upset, but it is not a time to handle these issues. Instead, be respectful and polite, saying, "This is not the right time to discuss this issue."

Rather than giving instruction on how to deal specifically with disgruntled parents, based on my experience I will simply introduce three prominent and recurring examples of issues that I came across and how I dealt with each one.

Case 1:
The "I Know More than the Coach" Scenario

We were in the middle of the season and were playing in a gym where all of the spectators sat in the balcony (this was a common setup in older gymnasiums thirty years ago). At the start of the third quarter, while I was going over my adjustments for the second half, someone tapped me on the shoulder. I turned and was surprised to see the father of my high scorer standing behind me. He said, "Coach, if you move my son from the guard position to the small forward, it will cause matchup problems and he will score more points." I guess that he thought he was Red Auerbach in the stands and knew more about the game than myself, so I told the parent to return to the balcony and I would make a move. Immediately, I sent a substitute in for the high scorer and kept him on the bench for the rest of the game. We won the game convincingly without his help, and the father never made any more suggestions for the rest of the season. Problem solved.

Case 2:
The "Why Isn't My Son Starting" Scenario

Prior to our first game of the season, I have each player rate their teammates based on what they have seen so far during the preseason. It's a great way to get the players' input on their peers, and it makes my job a heck of a lot easier because you learn right away which players are respected and which aren't. Leaders are developed this way. I would ask each of them to pick the starting team and then rate the other players from six to twelve. They never signed their names on the paper, but I could always tell who did the rating because most of them would always rate themselves higher. Once I compiled the ratings from all twelve players, I gave each of them a copy. Nine of ten times, the player's ratings correlated with my own. This is one tool that can be used with parents who ask why their sons are not starting. I normally would say, "Well, the rest of the team agrees with our starting team," and I would show them where their son was rated. Usually, this was the end of the problem.

Case 3:
The "Why Isn't My Son Getting Enough Shots?" Scenario

We lost a tough game one year, and, minutes after the game, my high scorer's mother came storming over to me to complain that her son was not getting enough shots. I told her that this was not the time to discuss this matter. The next day at practice, I had my stat manager give me a breakdown on our past seven games, including our last game. The stats showed that this student was averaging twenty shots a game, and the closest player behind him was taking only twelve. I made a photocopy of the stat sheet and gave it to our player with instructions to give it to his mother to sign and return to me. When the mother saw the stats, her complaints stopped.

The biggest problem that you will have is parental pressure on their own children. Most parents view this as legitimate parental concern, when in reality they are living their lives vicariously through their own sons and daughters. I have had numerous meetings with parents because of the pressure they put on their children.

During one game, at the half, one of my players came to me and said, "Please, coach, will you tell my father to shut up?" It seems that this parent would sit in the first row on the opposite side of the court, and every time his son would get the ball he would yell, "Shoot!" I told the player to bring his father to see me before our next practice.

When I met with the man, he was shocked when I suggested that he sit in the top row of the balcony and stop putting pressure on his son. Even so, he did as I suggested, and his son went on to have a great season. I was able to nip this problem in the bud before it escalated out of control, which can sometimes be the case if you let these issues drag on too long. It is your job as the head coach to solve these problems as soon as they surface so they don't persist. Your players look up to you, and they trust you to make the right decisions for them. In many cases, players are too young to do so themselves.

Polishing the Fundamentals Through Drillwork

Time-Tested Drills That Will Develop, Advance, and Hone the Skills of Your Players

Just as there are numerous fundamentals to work on each practice day, there are also certain drills that hone the fundamentals that should be incorporated for some type of consistency during practice time. As I emphasized in Chapter 2, when I discussed the idea that "practice makes perfect" when designing a practice plan, it is important to implement as many position-specific drills as possible. There is time for only so much practice, so as a coach you have to budget your time, a skill that comes with experience. Normally, guards and small forwards should work on explosive types of drills, where they can utilize their speed, while power forwards and centers should work on the low blocks, honing abilities such as boxing out, rebounding, and offensive and defensive positioning.

There are certain drills, however, the entire team can do together. These drills are more oriented toward the overall development of basic basketball skills and fundamentals, such as running the floor, boxing out, rebounding, shooting, and so forth. It is drills such as these that must be mastered and practiced enough

times during the course of the year because players use these skills in every game.

The following drills should be run at least two to three times a week during practice. Some of them are ageless. They were developed years ago and are time-tested techniques that can improve players' abilities. We would use them as much as possible, especially early in the season, before much of practice time was devoted to game planning and scouting opponents. For the full-court drills, the entire team would be involved, and we would repeat them for a time, usually either five or ten minutes a session, then move on. For position-specific drills, we broke the team into individual groups and used the side baskets as stations. Each group would work on a different drill. When the whistle was blown, we would rotate. It doesn't matter when you plan on working in these drills, as long as you work them into your schedule, because they not only improve a team but also give coaches the opportunity to evaluate the strengths and weaknesses of the team and individual players.

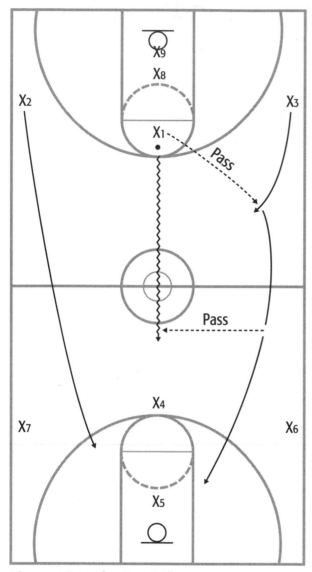

Figure 14.1 Twelve-Man Drill

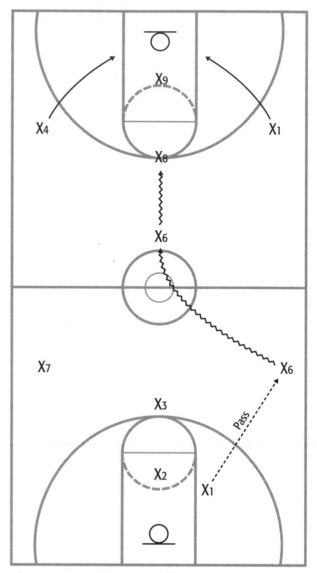

Figure 14.2 Twelve-Man Drill

FULL-COURT DRILLS

Twelve-Man Drill

This drill stresses the fast break (passing, rebounding, boxing out). It is used to start the practice and can be run with as many as fifteen players or as few as nine.

- Drill starts with X1 starting the fast break by passing to X2 or X3.
- X4 and X5 are in the I-defense.
- The rebounder passes to X6 and then sprints to take the position of X6.

- X6 dribbles to the middle and starts the fast break with X7 and the rebounder on the wing (fig. 14.1).
- The remainder of the players form the I-defense, while two players replace X7 and X6 at the wings (fig. 14.2).
- This drill can be repeated numerous times, until all players have each role on the court.

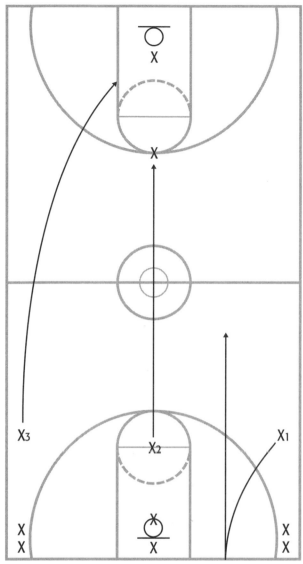

Figure 14.3 Upsala Drill

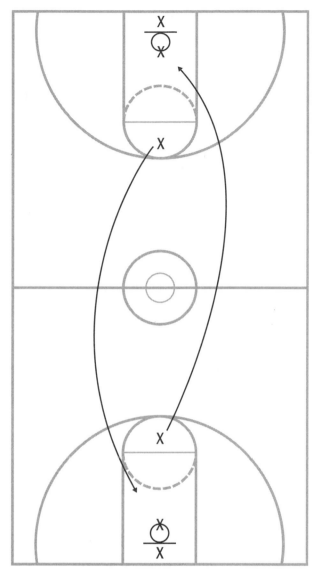

Figure 14.4 Pass and Layup Drill

Upsala Drill

This drill was on our agenda every practice. It is another fast-breaking conditioning drill.

- Each players is given a number.
- Coach calls a number, either 1, 2, or 3.
- The player whose number is called (for example, X1) must sprint and touch the back line before heading up court to fill a lane (fig. 14.3).
- On the previous break, whatever player rebounded continues in the drill, and the other two players form the I-defense.

Pass and Layup Drill

- Separate players into two groups.
- Each player faces another from opposite foul lines.
- Player 1 throws a two-handed overhead pass to player 2.
- Passer sprints up court to receive bounce pass from the receiver and go in for layup (fig. 14.4).
- Players switch lines.

Suicide Drill

This drill is used mainly for conditioning purposes. It develops quick movements and reaction times. You can time this drill or set it for a number of repetitions. The movement is done continuously, without stopping.

- All players line up on baseline facing down the court.
- On the coach's whistle, players sprint to the near foul line and backpedal back.
- Players then sprint to the half-court line and backpedal back.
- Players then sprint to the opposite foul line and backpedal back.
- Finally, players sprint the full court and backpedal back (fig. 14.5).

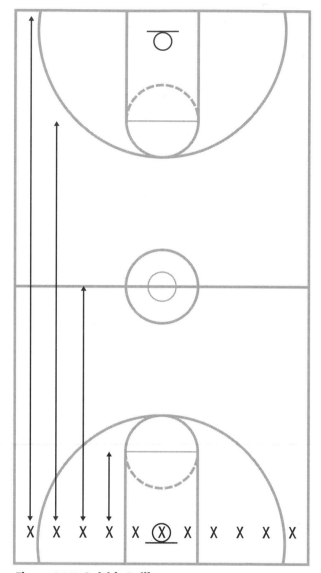

Figure 14.5 Suicide Drill

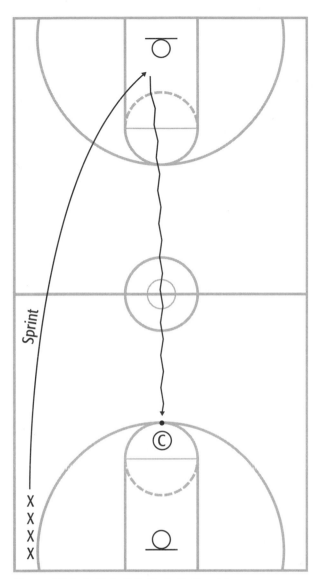

Figure 14.6 Roll-Ball Drill—Left-Hand Layup

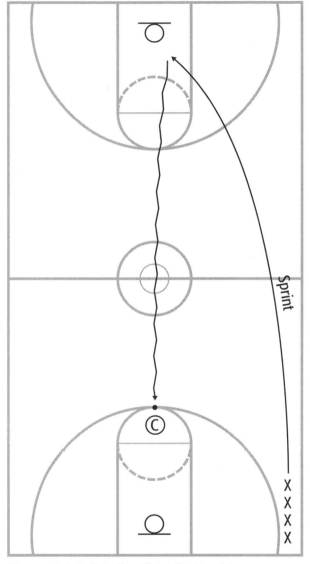

Figure 14.7 Roll-Ball Drill—Right-Hand Layup

Roll-Ball Drill

This drill is done with one player at a time. It develops quickness and speed while players learn how to race the length of the court and control their body for an easy score.

- Coach will roll the ball toward the opposite basket while the player waits on the baseline.
- Player must wait until the ball reaches the half-court line; then he sprints to catch up to it.

- Player picks up the ball, controls his dribble, and puts it in the basket for an easy layup (figs. 14.6 and 14.7).

Run-the-Floor Drill

We start practice with this drill every day. It replaces any type of lap running. It develops a player's quickness and agility. This drill is run without a basketball.

- Players are separated into three different lines, centers and power forwards on the foul line with guards and small forwards on each wing at one end of the court.
- The middle line sprints to opposite foul line and back, stopping once they get to the foul line.
- The two outside lines sprint to the baseline, run along the baseline around the basket, and end up at other end of the court (fig. 14.8).
- This drill may be timed or done for a certain amount of repetitions.

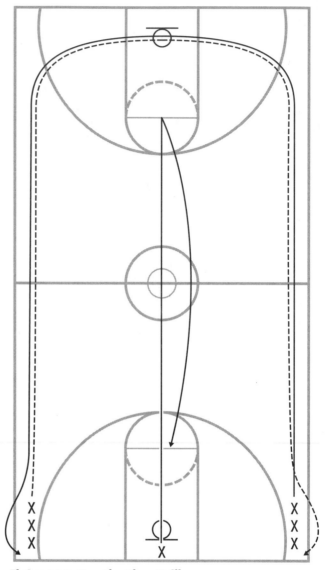

Figure 14.8 Run-the-Floor Drill

Box-Out into Fast-Break Drill

This drill develops the technique of boxing out and teaches players how to run the length of the floor after a rebound.

- The shooter takes a shot at the top of the key.
- X5 boxes shooter out.
- X3 dips in for rebound and delivers an outlet pass to X1.
- X1 passes to X2 as they run the middle of the floor.
- X1 fills one lane and X4 fills the other, while X2 brings the ball up court.
- X6 and X7 form the I-defense at the other end (fig. 14.9).
- Offensive team tries to score on defense.
- Rewards or points can be given to each team, depending on scores or stops.

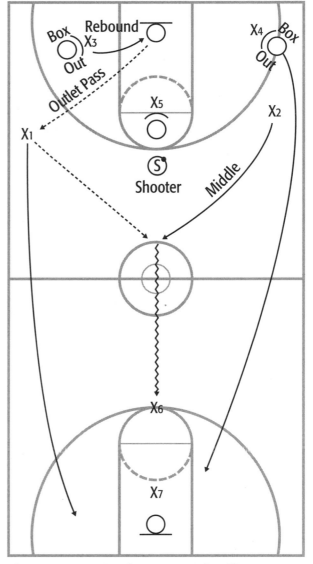

Figure 14.9 Box-Out into Fast-Break Drill

Conditioning Layup Drill

This is used as a fast-break drill. Two players run it at one time. It is designed to develop full-court movement and execution.

- X1 passes to X2 as an outlet.
- X2 dribbles the length of the court for a layup, then catches the ball before it hits the ground.
- X1 sprints the length of the court and touches the opposite foul line, then cuts to a wing to receive pass from X2.
- X1 dribbles the length of the court for a layup and catches the ball before it hits the ground (fig. 14.10).
- The process is repeated with two other players jumping up and running the drill.

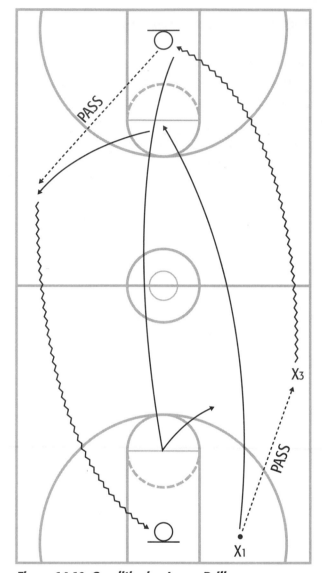

Figure 14.10 Conditioning Layup Drill

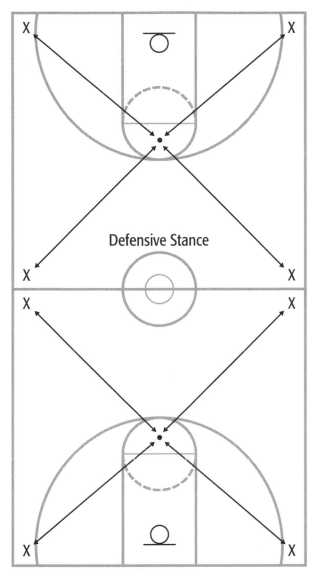

Figure 14.11 Sixty-Second Slide Drill

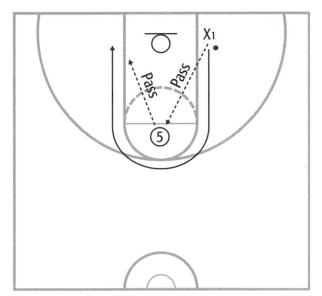

Figure 14.12 Peacock Drill, Left- and Right-Handed Layups

HALF-COURT DRILLS

Sixty-Second Slide Drill

This drill is used to teach the proper way of using the defensive slide.

- Players are separated into four groups and placed on the four corners of half-court.
- The center holds the ball on the ground while players in a defensive stance slide from each corner of half-court, touch the ball, and slide back (fig. 14.11).

- This drill should be done for one minute, as each player counts the number of times he touched the ball.

Peacock Drill

This drill is used to get proper angles to the basket for layups as well as execute the proper bounce pass. Two players drill at a time.

- X1 passes to X5 and then runs the complete foul line and receives a bounce pass from X5 for a left-handed layup.
- After making the shot, X1 passes to X5 and then runs the complete foul line, going the other way, and receives a bounce pass for a right-handed layup (fig. 14.12).

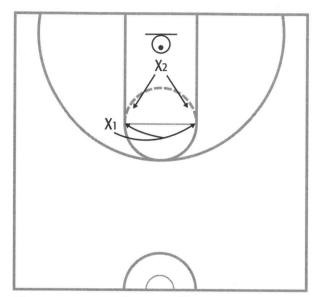

Figure 14.13 Beat-the-Pro Drill

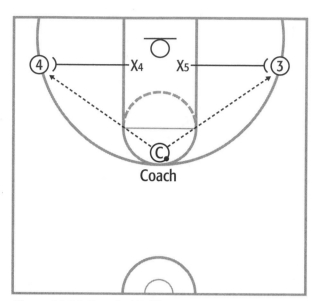

Figure 14.14 Box-Out Drill

Beat-the-Pro Drill

This drill is used to teach the proper form of a set jump shot, without coming off a dribble. One player at a time does the drill.

- X_1 starts at one elbow and receives a pass for a jump shot.
- X_1 then flashes to the other elbow and receives pass for a jump shot (fig. 14.13).
- The player gets one point per basket made.
- The "Pro" gets two points for every basket the player misses.
- The first player to reach twelve "wins."

Box-Out Drill

This drill is used to develop the proper technique of boxing out and getting a defensive rebound. It involves four players at a time.

- Coach passes the ball to either player 3 or 4, who will shoot a jump shot.
- On the release, X_4 and X_5 will make contact with the offensive player with their butt and hands, square their shoulders, grow wide, and keep their men from getting the rebound.
- After the ball hits the rim, X_4 and X_5 release and go for the ball (fig. 14.14).

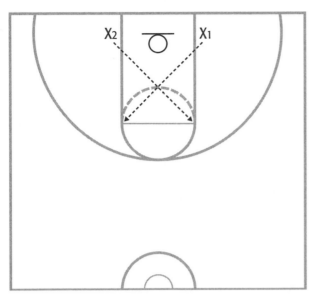

Figure 14.15 Half-Court Layup Drill

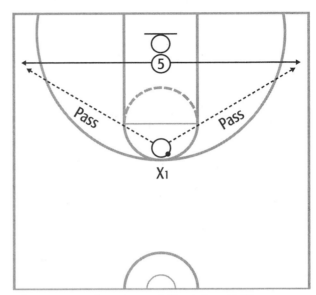

Figure 14.16 Sixty-Second Chest-Pass Drill

Half-Court Layup Drill

This drill is used to develop skills in seeing the ball, cutting to the basket, and making a layup. Two players at a time work on the drill.

- X1 rolls ball diagonally to elbow of free-throw line, chasing to pick it up at the elbow.
- X2 cuts diagonally to opposite elbow.
- X1 picks up ball and passes to X2 at the elbow.
- X1 cuts to basket and receives a bounce pass from X2 for easy layup (fig. 14.15).

Sixty-Second Chest-Pass Drill

This drill is used to work on the technique of a chest pass. One player at a time repeats.

- Player starts at one corner and receives a chest pass from the coach at the top of the key.
- After returning the pass, the player sprints the length of the baseline to the other corner to receive pass again.
- Process repeats.
- Players should square up and thrust the ball back, using chest muscles and stepping with their right feet (fig. 14.16).
- This drill runs nonstop for sixty seconds.

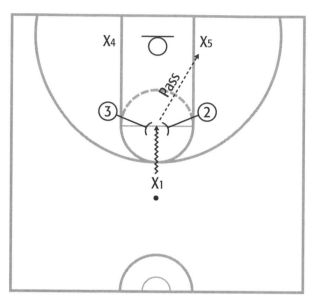

Figure 14.17 Pressure-Passing Drill

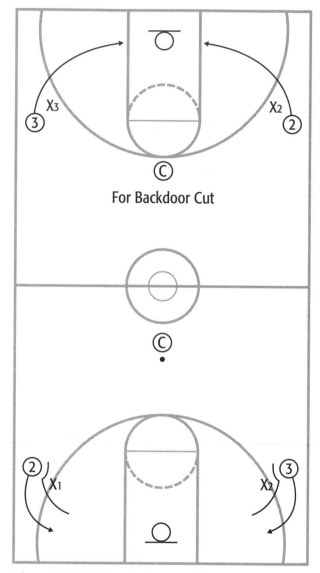

Figure 14.18 Defensive Deny Drill

Pressure-Passing Drill

Designed to prevent turnovers, this is one of the most important drills. It should be practiced every day.

- X1 dribbles to the foul line and is trapped by X2 and X3.
- X1 must protect the ball and constantly pivot for three seconds.
- He then must try to pass the ball to X4 or X5.
- On pass to either X4 or X5, the opposite player flashes to guard him and prevent him from scoring (fig. 14.17).

Defensive Deny Drill

This drill is used to stress defending the backdoor cut. It is another drill that should be part of every practice.

- The coach attempts to pass to either 2 or 3 while X3 and X2 purposely overplay them to deny the pass.
- Unable to receive the pass, 2 and 3 cut backdoor.
- X2 opens to his right with his eyes on the passer and looks for intercept.
- X3 opens to his left and eyes the passer, looking for intercept (fig. 14.18).

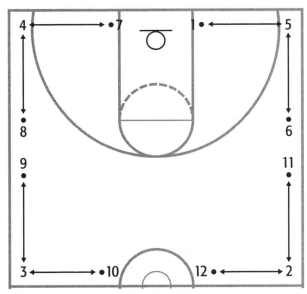

Figure 14.19 Corner-Passing Drill

Corner-Passing Drill

This is a reflex drill that consists of twelve men, three in each corner.

- 4 is in the corner, 7 and 8 have basketballs.
- 4 turns to face 7 as 7 passes to 4.
- 4 passes back to 7 in time to receive pass from 8.
- 4 passes back to 8.
- Each player must get in the corner for one minute (fig. 14.19).

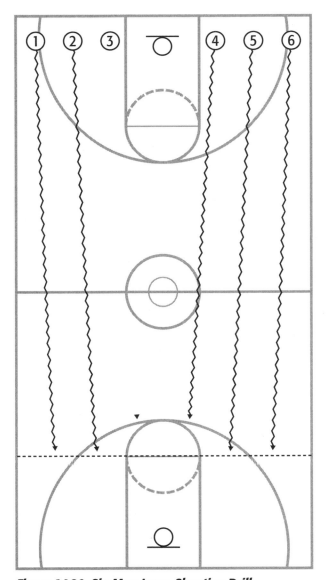

Figure 14.20 Six-Man Jump-Shooting Drill

Six-Man Jump-Shooting Drill

This drill is used with six players in a full-court situation and develops shooting skills.

- Coach blows the whistle and 1 starts to dribble.
- When 1 is at half-court, whistle sounds and 2 starts to dribble.
- Repeat until all six shooters take jump shots at the three-point area (fig.14.20).

Coach's Note: Centers shoot at the foul-line area.

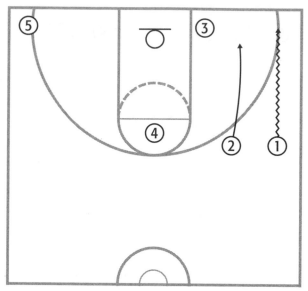

Figure 14.21 Five-Man Defensive Drill

Five-Man Defensive Drill

This drill is used with five players in a half-court situation. It develops both offensive and defensive skills.

- 1 dribbles to baseline, then passes to 3.
- 2 plays tight defense "nose on ball."
- 3 passes to 4, who will rock step into a jump shot.
- 3 races to the shooter and challenges the shot, then boxes out the shooter.
- 4 retrieves the ball after the shot and passes to 5.

- 5 drives the baseline to the basket.
- 4 positions himself on the baseline and takes the charge (fig. 14.21).

Reflex Drill

- Two lines of five players each, one on baseline and one on foul line extended
- Xs have basketballs; Os do not.
- Os have backs to Xs.
- Players in X tap ball, and all Os turn to face the ball and make the catch (fig. 14.22).
- Players switch responsibilities and drill repeats.

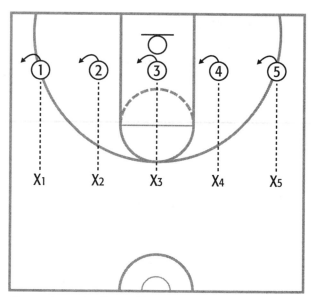

Figure 14.22 Reflex Drill

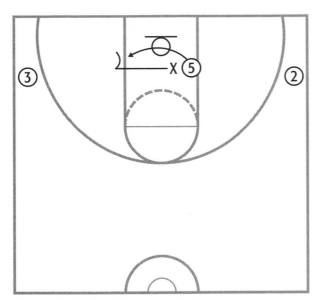

Figure 14.23 Post Defensive Drill

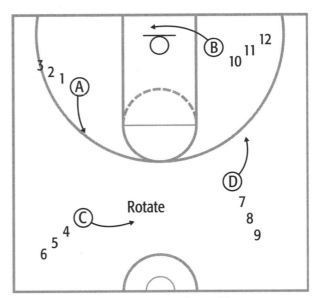

Figure 14.24 Four-Corner Passing Drill

Post Defensive Drill

- Two offensive players are used to feed the ball down low to the post player.
- X guards the post man.
- He is to front the post man and prevent him from getting the ball.
- The ball is passed by the two feeders, but must be thrown in at the side position, not at the top of the key.
- The defender must keep positioning between his man and the ball and continue to front the post player (fig. 14.23).

Four-Corner Passing Drill

This dribble works on the technique and repetition of all possible passes in basketball.

- A dribbles and makes a two-handed chest pass after his pivot to C.
- C makes an over-the-head pass to D.
- D makes a bounce pass to B.
- B makes a two-handed chest pass to A (fig. 14.24).
- The cycle continues until all players have made each of the passes.

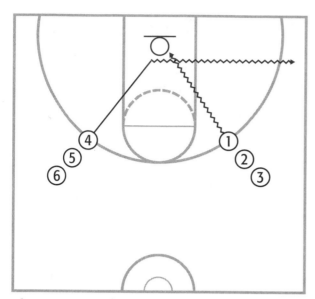

Figure 14.25 Angle Layup Drill for Guards

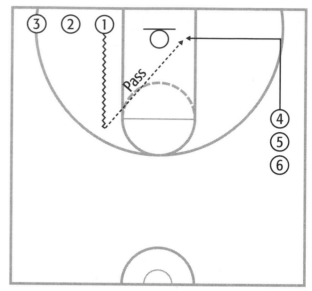

Figure 14.26 Angle Layup Drill for Forwards

Angle Layup Drill for Guards

This is the most common drill to develop the fundamentals of layups.

- 1 drives for a layup.
- 4 rebounds and dribbles parallel to baseline and passes to 2.
- 2 cuts to basket to make a layup (fig. 14.25).
- Players switch sides and work both the right and left sides.

Angle Layup Drill for Forwards

- 1 dribbles to foul line and bounce passes to 4.
- 4 makes a 90-degree cut for the baseline layup.
- Players switch sides and work both the right and left sides (fig. 14.26).

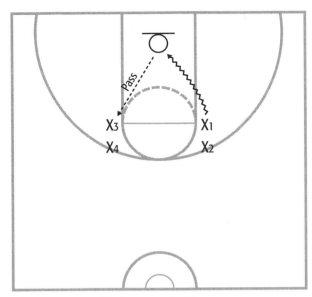

Figure 14.27 Dribble Layup Drill

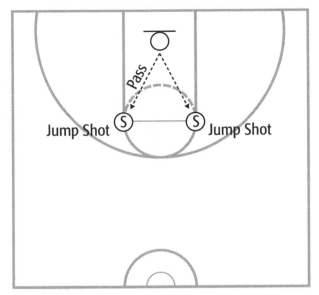

Figure 14.28 Square-to-Basket Jump-Shot Drill

MISCELLANEOUS FUNDAMENTAL DRILLS

Dribble Layup Drill

- X1 dribbles for a right-hand layup, takes ball from net, and passes to X3.
- X3 dribbles and takes a left-handed layup, then passes to X2.
- Players switch lines (fig. 14.27).

Square-to-Basket Jump-Shot Drill

- Take jump shot at the foul line.
- Race in to get rebound for a right-handed layup.
- Move ball to opposite elbow and square up for jump shot.
- Race in to get rebound for a left-handed layup (fig. 14.28)
- Repeat drill five times.

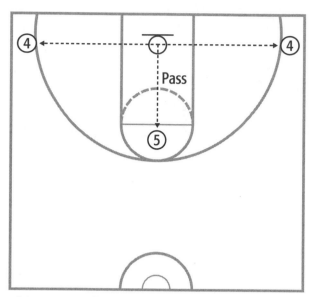

Figure 14.29 Three-Point Shot-Drill for Forwards

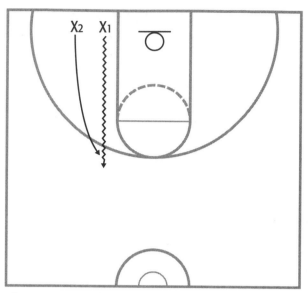

Figure 14.30 Defensive Flick Drill

Three-Point Shot-Drill for Forwards

- Forward shoots three-pointer from the corner and follows his shot.
- Retrieves the ball and passes to teammate at the foul line.
- He then sprints to the opposite corner, receives the ball from teammate, squares to the corner, and shoots a three-pointer (fig. 14.29).

Defensive Flick Drill

- Two lines of players behind the baseline.
- X_1 dribbles the ball to foul line, while X_2 attacks the ball from behind for the steal.

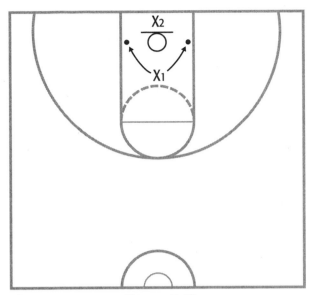

Figure 14.31 Two-Ball Layup Drill

Two-Ball Layup Drill

- X1 shoots right- and left-handed layups.
- X2 replaces the balls (fig. 14.31).
- Players rotate.

Three-on-Three Drill

- Excellent drill to end practice; players seem to enjoy this type of setup.
- Generates tremendous competition.
- Players get paired up into four three-man teams by the coach.
- First two teams play half-court basketball for one point while another team waits under the basket.
- If offensive team scores, they stay on the court and start again at the top of the three-point line.
- The waiting team sprints on to defend them.
- If the defensive team gains possession, they remain on the floor.
- Play starts even if the defensive team is not ready.
- The scoring is up to twenty-one.
- Some type of reward must be given to the winning team—they are exempt from running or conditioning.

Perfect Practice Makes Perfect Teams

Developing a Consistent and Productive Practice Plan That Will Keep Your Team on Track the Entire Season

've always been a firm believer that how a team practices is how it plays. As a coach, whatever you do in the two hours or so you have with your team each day will directly carry over into game-day performance. One of the most influential coaches I've known over the years is George Blaney, who is now an assistant at the University of Connecticut. When he was head coach at Holy Cross College in Massachusetts, I had the opportunity to observe some of his practices. Setting aside the differences in talent and ability from high school to college, I was most impressed with how focused his players were, how in tune they were to what was going on. Beside their evident hustle and shooting and jumping abilities, it seemed as though nobody made a mistake, and the few times they did, they corrected themselves. Coach Blaney didn't have to reprimand any of them. I tried to emulate this as much as possible with my own players because I realized that you cannot teach someone ability; you can only teach them how to use it.

I learned that if players are comfortable responding to different situations and, most important, adversity in practice, they will be comfortable in games. Unfortunately, poise and self-control in pressure situations are not qualities you can coach. However, players can learn them through repetition in practice. A coach can present players with as many different variables as possible (throw the book at them, as it is called) and see how they respond. Chances are you'll find your "go-to" guys by the way they respond in practice.

I always understood the importance of a "good" practice, but I suppose I never comprehended the benefits of a "great" practice. That was what I strove for every day we took the court. Now, obviously, the law of percentages says that you can never always have a great practice—and there are days you have to forget quickly— but if you are consistent as a coach and give your players a routine to follow as soon as they hit the court, there is a strong chance you'll have great workouts. One thing I learned from my years of coaching is that routine teaches discipline and discipline provides results. I remember the great John Wooden saying, "Discipline of others isn't punishment. You discipline to help, to improve, to correct, and to prevent. Not to punish, humiliate or retaliate."

Before each season started, I spent a lot of time outlining what I wanted to accomplish in each practice session. You could say that I had my goals and my objectives down to a precise, well-thought-out lesson plan. I had my schedule and routine of events that I would follow. The hardest part was not deviating from these plans, trying my best, and staying on task with what I was doing. For example, if I wanted to accomplish shooting against a 1-3-1 zone or breaking a half-court trap on a particular day, I didn't leave the court until I felt we had done it successfully, until we had built enough repetitions and consistency to complete the day and work toward tomorrow. This is the key to coaching—you have to get better every day. It's like climbing a ladder. Every rung counts until you get to the top. If you miss one, you're bound to slip off and have to start all over again. I tried my best to avoid slipping.

In most cases, the basketball season starts the day after Thanksgiving, which is when the football season ends. The first game is usually scheduled for the third week in December, which leaves approximately one month (or thirty days) to prepare for the season. In this chapter, I describe in detail everything we accounted for up to that first game day—every drill, every fundamental, everything we needed to work on to improve ourselves and get to the point where we were ready to compete. We introduced at least one new fundamental for each practice session.

I have a couple of key philosophies when it comes to conducting a perfect practice. First, I held practice for two hours—nothing more, nothing less. Anything less is too short. Anything longer and the players begin to lose focus—they are high school students, and there's a lot more going on in their lives socially and academically than that of professional or college players. For those two hours, though, I tried to make practice as intense as possible—all hustle, hardly any talking, and little confusion. My players knew they had to come prepared to practice every day; I treated it just like an actual game. Like a lesson plan, I stated my objectives, we accomplished them, and we moved on. There could not be any wasted time. The tempo of a practice should emphasize complete discipline. Conditioning is built into a successful practice—it is all basketball-related. The only time we did conditioning drills like sprints or suicides was for punishment. Otherwise, it was a waste of time. We didn't waste time running sprints at the end of practice, either. For players to get into game shape, they have to practice movements they execute in the game. If you do this the right way, you won't need to condition because the practice itself serves as conditioning.

We held our varsity, junior varsity, and freshmen tryouts three days before our first official practice. After we made our cuts, each level was cut to fifteen players. Those forty-five players were then reduced to twelve a team by the start of the preseason. The following is a breakdown, time by time, of what our practices looked like for the first thirty days of the preseason, starting with day four.

Day 4

4:00   Welcome all players; outline team rules, goals, and expectations.

4:10   Fundamental of the day (for example, defensive flick—any time a defensive player is trailing the offensive dribbler, always attack the ball from behind).

4:15   Warm-up drill (for example, run-the-floor drill).

4:30   Discipline drill. The coach blows the whistle and points to bleacher area. Players sprint to that area. The last player to reach the area does ten pushups.

4:35   Shooting demonstration. The coach reviews all ten shooting fundamentals as players practice shooting.

5:00   Fast-break drill.

5:30   Twelve-man drill, to teach the fast break, boxing-out, rebounding, outlet pass, pass to the middle, and perimeter shooting. This is done all in one and at a quick tempo.

5:50   Pressure free throw. The coach selects a player to shoot a free throw. If the player makes the shot, the team has ten minutes of free time to practice free throws. If the player misses, all players must run fifteen laps around the gym. (The drill repeats until practice ends on a completed free throw.)

Day 5

4:00   Shooting practice. Coaches correct errors.

4:15   Peacock layup drill.

4:25   Two-ball drill.

4:30   Run-the-floor drill.

4:35   Upsala drill.

4:45   Fundamental of the day (for example, always meet the ball on a pass; don't let the ball meet you).

4:50   Conditioning and defensive drill.

5:00   Pressure passing drill.

5:15   Defensive deny and open for backdoor cut. Passing under pressure teaches the player to pivot, then pass. Never stay stationary. It also teaches how to deny the ball one pass away and how to open to the ball to intercept the backdoor pass.

5:30 Twelve-man drill.

5:50 Pressure free throw.

Day 6

4:00 Run-the-floor drill.

4:10 Shooting drill—"Beat the Pro" (for example, players take jump shots from each elbow of the free throw. They get one point for every made shot; the "Pro" gets two points for every missed shot. Winner is first to get to twenty-one).

4:30 Five-man defensive drill.

4:45 Boxing-out drill.

5:00 Four-corner passing drill.

5:15 Fundamental of the day (for example, changing speed while running off a pick and setting a pick).

5:20 Pressure man-to-man defense.

5:50 Pressure free throw.

Day 7

4:00 Run-the-floor drill.

4:10 Work on post moves for center and big forwards; guards and small forwards practice three-point shooting.

4:30 Fundamental of the day (for example, always pick up all out-of-bounds balls as if they went out of bounds off your opponent).

4:35 Sixty-second defensive slide drill.

4:45 Drawing the charge. Stress how to prevent getting hurt and moving backward when contact is made.

5:00 Fast break and fast-break offense.

5:50 Pressure free throw.

Day 8

4:00 Run-the-floor drill.

4:10 "Beat-the-Pro" shooting drill.

4:20 Conditioning and defensive drill.

4:30 Fundamental of the day (for example, the backdoor-cut rule: if a player takes two steps toward the hoop, he must continue to make cut).

4:40 Explanation of one series man-to-man offense.

5:40 Three-on-three basketball tournament until practice ends.

Day 9

4:00 Run-the-floor drill.

4:10 Boxing-out and outlet-pass drill.

4:20 Upsala drill.

4:30 Explanation of two-series offense.

5:30 Twelve-man drill.

5:50 Pressure free throw.

Day 10

4:00 Run-the-floor drill.

4:10 Fast-break offense.

4:30 Man-to-man pressure defense.

5:00 Defensive tap play.

5:10 Explanation of three-series offense.

5:50 Fundamental of the day (for example, always stop the advance of the ball. Tie up the rebounder to prevent outlet pass to fast break. Always force the advancing ball to the sidelines and away from the middle).

5:55 Pressure free throw.

Day 11

4:00 Run-the-floor drill.

4:10 Explain zone defenses and teach proper slides on the 2-1-2 zone.

4:30 Teach the 1-3-1 zone offense and the stack offense.

5:00 Full-court scrimmage with 1-3-1 offense against the 2-1-2 defense. Loser does pushups or extra form of conditioning.

5:50 Fundamental of the day (for example, freeing yourself for an inbound pass).

5:55 Pressure free throw.

Day 12

4:00 Run-the-floor drill.

4:10 Man-to-man out-of-bounds plays.

4:30 Zone out-of-bounds plays.

4:45 Side out-of-bounds plays.

5:00 Fundamental of the day (for example, fronting the shooter).

5:05 Scrimmage. Man-to-man pressure defense with one-, two-, and three-series offenses.

5:50 Pressure free throw.

Day 13

4:00 Run-the-floor drill.

4:10 Shooting drill.

4:30 Fundamental of the day (for example, how to avoid being boxed out).

4:35 Pressure-pass drill.

4:50 One-on-one penetration drill.

5:00 Double-motion offense.

5:50 Pressure free throw.

Day 14

4:00 Run-the-floor drill.

4:10 Pressure man-to-man defense (stress hitting the gap for a steal and meeting the ball on defense if your man does not meet the ball on offense).

4:30 Zone motion offense.

5:30 Fundamental of the day (for example, ripping the ball away from defensive rebounder if he brings the ball down).

5:35 Jump-shot-square-to-hoop drill, from elbow of the free-throw line.

5:50 Pressure free throw.

Day 15

4:00 Run-the-floor drill.

4:10 Layup drill (twelve shots from the right, twelve from the left, and twelve from the middle).

4:30 Pressure defense.

5:30 Fundamental of the day (for example, never foul on a difficult or low-percentage shot).

5:35 Review of out-of-bounds plays.

5:50 Pressure free throw.

Day 16

4:00 Run-the-floor drill.

4:10 Zone motion offense.

4:30 Scrimmage. Man-to-man defense and zone motion offense.

5:10 Scrimmage. 2-1-2 and 3-2 zone defense and zone motion offense.

5:40 Fundamental of the day (for example, calling time-out when falling out of bounds on a key possession).

5:45 Each player takes pressure free throw; on miss, he runs five laps and then gets back on line.

Day 17

4:00 Run-the-floor drill.

4:10 Corner-passing drill.

4:30 Fundamental of the day (for example, the best pass on a fast break is the bounce pass, when the man is cutting to the basket).

4:35 Review all offenses, out-of-bounds plays, and defensive fundamentals.

5:50 Pressure free throw.

Day 18

4:00 Run-the-floor drill.

4:10 Fundamental of the day (for example, never leave your man unless the ball leaves his fingers).

4:15 Out-of-bounds plays.

4:30 Post work for centers and big forwards; three-point-shot work for guards and small forwards.

4:45 Review Falcon full-court-press offense.

5:00 Review Columbia half-court-press offense.

5:15 Review fast-break offense.

5:50 Pressure free throw.

Day 19

4:00 Run-the-floor drill.

4:10 Box-and-one offense.

4:30 Diamond zone offense.

5:00 Stunting offenses.

5:25 Stunting defense.

5:50 Fundamental of the day (for example, when receiving an outlet pass, pivot to avoid a charge; rebounder must pivot before passing to outlet).

5:55 Pressure free throw.

Day 20

4:00 Run-the-floor drill.

4:10 Deny-the-ball defensive drill.

4:30 "Beat-the-Pro" shooting drill.

4:45 Upsala drill.

5:00 Controlled scrimmage. (Select two captains for each team; choose sides; twelve-point game by ones; best two of three wins; loser does pushups or extra conditioning exercise.)

Day 21

4:00 Run-the-floor drill.

4:10 Shooting-of-a-dribble drill.

4:30 Fundamental of the day (for example, on pressure defense, when guarding the man with the ball, give a five-second count to alert official—count for the official).

4:35 Fast-break offense, stressing players shouting "Outlet" and "Middle."

5:00 Work on zone offenses and defenses.

5:50 Pressure free throws.

Day 22

4:00 Run-the-floor drill.

4:10 Fundamental of the day (for example, look for the defender before making the pass).

4:15 "Beat-the-Pro" shooting drill.

4:30 Man-to-man offenses and pressure man-to-man defenses.

5:30 Review all out-of-bounds plays.

5:45 Each player shoots pressure jump shot from foul line; missed shots equal laps.

Day 23

4:00 Run-the-floor drill.

4:10 Fundamental of the day (for example, on defense, always keep your feet on the ground unless the ball is already in the air and you can block it).

4:15 Review basic defensive rotation on baseline by opponent.

4:45 Separation drill. (Teams are separated into two groups. The coach calls offensive play, and both teams run the offense at the same time. Player who messes up the offense is replaced by substitute.)

5:45 Pressure free throw.

Day 24

4:00 Run-the-floor drill.

4:10 "Beat-the-Pro" shooting drill.

4:30 Teams A and B scrimmage; stress fast break and boxing out.

5:45 Each player shoots jump shot from corner; number of misses equals number of laps.

Day 25

4:00 Run-the-floor drill.

4:10 Fundamental of the day (for example, on defense always keep one eye on your man and one eye on the ball—"see man, see ball").

4:15 Work post moves for centers and big forwards; work three-point shooting for guards and small forwards.

4:35 Fast-break offense from man-to-man defense and 2-1-2 zone defense.

5:50 Pressure free throw.

Day 26

4:00 Run-the-floor drill.

4:10 Fundamental of the day (for example, always spin when your opponent tries to box you out).

4:15 Fast-break offense.

4:45 "Beat-the-Pro" shooting drill.

5:00 Review out-of-bounds plays.

5:50 Pressure free throw; team captain picks player.

Day 27
(day before the first game)

4:00 Shoot-around (free throws, three-pointers, pivots, turnarounds).

4:30 Scouting report and film work.

5:00 Game plan installation; review of all significant plays or sets.

6:00 Rest.

APPENDIX

Coach Bill Kuchar's Gallery of New Jersey Championship Teams and Players

Coach Bill Kuchar with the Wardlaw-Hartridge 1998–1999 champions.

Coach Bill Kuchar, left, receives the Horseshoe Championship trophy from Sister Celestia, principal of St. Anthony's High School, Jersey City, as Tony Nicodemo, athletic director of St. Mary's and Tony Nocera, athletic director of St. Anthony's, look on. Both played for St. Michael's College in Vermont and both were 1,000-point scorers.

Coach Kuchar of Wardlaw-Hartridge Prep presents a 1,000-point ball to Mike Campbell, All State First Team in basketball, baseball and soccer.

Garry Witts (dark uniform), of St. Joe's went on to Holy Cross and then on to the NBA Washington Bullets.

Kevin Wall, outstanding player at St. Mary's High School, Jersey City. Wall was the center on the school's state championship team. During the state tournament, he went to the foul line (with the game on the line) and made one foul shot with his right hand and one foul shot with his left, a feat that left the standing-room-only crowd stunned!

Wardlaw's Ken Kaye was not only a 1,000-point scorer, he also broke (and still holds) Middlesex County's three-point shooting record.

Coach Kuchar presents the scouting award to John Hoops for twenty years of outstanding service. Hoops was an outstanding basketball player for Middlebury College in Vermont.

Cocaptain Leo Casale, left, and Captain Luke Griffin of St. Mary's 1975 state champions. Griffin went on to star at St. Joseph's in Pennsylvania and was later drafted by the 76ers.

Ken Miller, outstanding player on offense and defense and captain of the 1969 St. Mary's state championship team.

Joe Camillery's jersey was retired when he became the first 1,000-point scorer in St. Mary's history. Coach Kuchar looks on with St. Peter's College head coach Don Kennedy as Camillery contemplates continuing his career at St. Peter's College.

Craig Ross, leading scorer in Hudson County, New Jersey, and member of St. Mary's 1969 state champions, is presented a 1,000-point ball by Coach Kuchar.

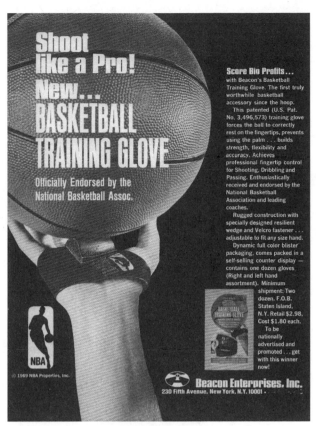

Basketball shooting glove invented by Coach Kuchar forces the ball onto the fingertips for better control.

Joe Camillery, St. Mary's first 1,000-point scorer, and basketball and baseball star Vin Petrarca hold their trophies while Coach Bill Kuchar and Father Griffith, pastor at St. Mary's High School, look on. Camillery accepted a basketball scholarship to St. Peter's College in Jersey City, New Jersey.

Index

About the Author

By the time he retired from coaching basketball in 1999, Bill Kuchar was the fourth-winningest high school coach in New Jersey history. With an astonishing record of 659 wins and 275 losses, Kuchar won eight state championships, as well as seventeen league titles, in a career that spanned forty years.

Born and raised in the basketball hotbed of Jersey City, New Jersey, Kuchar graduated from Dickinson High School in Hudson County, starring in basketball, baseball, and cross-country. He went on to accept a full scholarship to Division 2, St. Michael's College, in Vermont, where he was a three-year varsity starter and 1,000-point scorer during his career.

Kuchar got his first head coaching job in 1959, when he was just twenty-four years old, at Saint Mary's High School in Jersey City. (The program, under a different coach, won only two games the year before he got there.) Kuchar stayed for seventeen seasons, winning four parochial state championships during his tenure, the first coming in 1967. His 1974–1975 team was recognized as the number-one team in New Jersey and broke a school record with twenty-five wins. He won a total of 276 games at St. Mary's and also served as the school's baseball coach and athletic director.

From there, Kuchar turned St. Joseph's of Metuchen into a hoops powerhouse, winning 210 games in twelve seasons to go along with three conference championships. In 1983, he was named the Middlesex County Coach of the Year. After a one-year stint at St. Pius in Piscataway, Kuchar finished his career at the Wardlaw-Hartridge School in Edison, where he once again turned a dormant program that had won just four games in the previous three seasons into a four-time state championship dynasty, posting undefeated seasons in 1994 and 1996.

Throughout his career, Kuchar has helped 130 players continue their basketball careers at the collegiate level. Some of the more prominent players he has coached include Jimmy Boylan, who went on to win a national championship at Marquette University in 1976, and Garry Witts, who broke Bob Cousy's career field-goal percentage (54 percent) at Holy Cross College from 1980 to 1985.

After retiring, Kuchar moved to Clark Township, New Jersey, where he has served for five years on the township council as a councilman and one term as council president. He was inducted into the Hudson County Hall of Fame in 2000 as a player/coach and is also the founder and chief executive officer of the All-Star Sports Center chain, with six stores in northern New Jersey.